"*Sacred Love* captures your attenti[on] ... you won't be able to put it down! 1[...] ... she exposes a subject we all deal with—God's unconditional love regardless of your circumstances. What matters most? Loving God with all our hearts and accepting His eternal love."

BOB BUFORD
Author, *Halftime* and *Drucker & Me*
Founder, the Halftime Institute

"A story of hope and redemption, *Sacred Love* is a real-life account of God's pursuit of love for us, even when we prefer to be self-sufficient. Claudia's love stories with the Prince of Peace and eventually with a godly husband are woven together with a fresh look at Scripture. Readers will enjoy the humor, honesty, and life application while being reminded that God truly loves us."

JOHNNY HUNT
Senior Pastor, First Baptist Church of Woodstock, Georgia
Author, *Building Your Spiritual Resume, Shoe Leather Christianity,*
Building Your Leadership Resume, and *Wisdom from the Scriptures Vol. 1*

"Reading *Sacred Love* will make you happy inside! Whether you are single, married, widowed, or divorced, Claudia's five-star story will speak to that part of you that longs to know God really loves you and will meet you in a very personal way, right where you are."

JAN SILVIOUS
Author, *Fool-Proofing Your Life, Big Girls Don't Whine,*
and *Same Life, New Story*

"Checkmate. I am far from a chess expert, but I know that checkmate declares either victory or defeat. Claudia Cantrell's inspiring book, *Sacred Love,* lovingly shows women and men alike how to negotiate the pieces of singleness to victory. Readers are cleverly drawn into Claudia's personal love story that takes you through surprise attacks by Satan, a skillful player, to King Jesus' final declaration, 'Checkmate, you are Mine.'"

DR. JOHN HULL
Lead Pastor, Eastside Baptist Church, Marietta, Georgia

♥

SACRED LOVE

*a journey of singleness,
belonging, and finding true love*

♥

SACRED LOVE

*a journey of singleness,
belonging, and finding true love*

BY CLAUDIA CANTRELL WITH KIM P. DAVIS

NEW HOPE®
PUBLISHERS
Gospel-Centered. Missions-Driven.

New Hope® Publishers
PO Box 12065
Birmingham, AL 35202-2065
NewHopePublishers.com
New Hope Publishers is a division of WMU®.

Library of Congress Cataloging-in-Publication Data

Names: Cantrell, Claudia, 1957- author.
Title: Sacred love : a journey of singleness, belonging, and finding true
   love / by Claudia Cantrell, with Kim P. Davis.
Description: Birmingham, AL : New Hope Pubishers, 2017.
Identifiers: LCCN 2016034015 (print) | LCCN 2016043907 (ebook) | ISBN
   9781625915146 (sc) | ISBN 9781596699670 (e-book)
Subjects: LCSH: Cantrell, Claudia, 1957- | Christian biography--United States.
Classification: LCC BR1725.C2345 A3 2017 (print) | LCC BR1725.C2345 (ebook) |
   DDC 277.3/083092 [B] --dc23
LC record available at https://lccn.loc.gov/2016034015

ISBN-13: 978-1-62591-514-6

N174112 • 0217 • 2.5M1

You are My servant, I have chosen you and not rejected you.
Do not fear, for I am with you; do not anxiously look about you,
for I am your God. I will strengthen you, surely I will help you,
surely I will uphold you with My righteous right hand.

Isaiah 41:9–10

To my Prince of Peace,
Jesus Christ,
and to my earthly prince,
David—
both of whom chose me
and show me
unconditional love
every day.

Table of Contents

Acknowledgments

David, I want to thank you for believing in me. You are my earthly prince and husband who shows me unconditional love, inspires me, and encourages me every day. I respect and love you more than anyone. You are my best friend and confidant.

Katie, my "daughter," thank you for being like my own. You accepted me from the beginning and have shown me unconditional love. You have allowed me to be your "mother" and dear friend.

To my "daughter" in heaven who is with our Savior—Kelly—I am thankful you saw something in me from the start and encouraged your dad to seek me out.

Thank you, my wonderful prayer warriors, who have prayed diligently for this book daily as it was being written. Amy Brown, Lori Lee, Tracy Arntzen, Diane Rose, Gertrude Steinhauer, Elizabeth Weatherby, and Susanna Hafner—you are my dear friends.

To the pilot readers—David, Katie Cantrell, Maddison Askren, Lori Lee, and Millie White—I appreciate your advice, encouragement, friendship, and support.

A special thank you, Kim Davis, for your excellence in writing. I could not have completed this book without you.

Thank you to the many friends who have loved, supported, and prayed for me throughout the years.

Thank you to New Hope Publishers for their hard work to get this book in the hands of women (and men!) looking for hope.

Mostly, I want to thank my Lord and Savior, Jesus Christ, who left His throne in heaven to come to earth and die a sinless death on a Cross for my salvation. Due to His resurrected life and my trust in Him, I will live with Him in heaven throughout eternity.

CHAPTER I

From Rags to Bridal Gown

At 50 years old, I had attended more than my fair share of weddings, none my own. Regardless of a person's marital state, there's something about hearing the wedding march that brings goose bumps and unexplained tears while getting a glimpse of the tuxedo-clad groom straining to see his bride. Turning, the guests see the radiant bride begin her slow descent down the aisle as she searches for her waiting groom.

Oh, the magnificent and breathtaking dress! No wonder there are reality television shows about picking out the perfect bridal gown. The white, charmeuse lightweight fabric that is satin-like to touch; the ballgown bodice that fits tightly around the waistline, leading to a full and flowing floor-length skirt; the modest bateau neckline that follows the curve of the collarbone to the very tip of the shoulders; the scattered gemstones that sparkle in the candlelight; the chapel-length train that falls elegantly around her shoulders and down her back—all dazzling components of the bride's attire. Yet the most beautiful thing to see is the pure joy on the face of the bride as she anticipates reaching the one who unconditionally loves her enough to even die for her.

Imagine another scenario with me. This bride believes in her bridegroom. Her dreams, hopes, and preparations have led to this day, although she could have missed it. Because she has no parents, she has no dowry. In fact, when the man of her dreams found her, she was dressed in filthy rags. She was not fit to be in the presence of her groom, especially when she found out that he was the king's son. The prince! But he lifted her out of the ashes. He made it possible for her to have a long, hot bath, a manicure and pedicure, and a new hairstyle. He had the finest seamstresses custom design her gown that was whiter than new-fallen snow. The bridegroom gave her everything. All that she had to give him was herself. No one had bothered to look her way before, so her purity is intact. She at least has that to give. And even if she had been impure, this prince is like no other. He would love her anyway. Why? Because he chose her. She is the one who makes his heart skip a beat.

As believers in Christ, we are His bride. This scenario may be hard for a man to imagine, but women can easily picture the scene. In Isaiah 61:10, the prophet draws an analogy of celebration between God's followers and a bride.

> I will rejoice greatly in the LORD, My soul will exult in my God; for He has clothed me with garments of salvation, He has wrapped me with a robe of righteousness, as a bridegroom decks himself with a garland, and as a bride adorns herself with her jewels.

Later in Isaiah 62:5, the theme continues with, "And as the bridegroom rejoices over the bride, so your God will rejoice over you."

I became a Christian as a child, but up until my late forties, I had a hard time believing and living like I was the bride of Christ. I had not fully grasped that the moment I decided to follow Jesus, He freed me from sin, restored me to who I was created to be, and clothed me in His righteousness. In other words, Christ alone makes His followers right with God. He gives us a new name—Christian—and pours out His love on us. He makes a covenant with us that can't be broken—marriage for life. He will not walk out on us. It's against His character. Our apparel is salvation, and only He can adorn us.

When I came to the end of myself through brokenness at middle age, I fully surrendered everything to Jesus. My surrender required full and unwavering trust in Him. I relinquished what I thought I wanted and stopped trying to manipulate things to go my way. All my desires and dreams were left at His feet. Jesus is trustworthy. When I finally gave Him all of me, I was filled with peace and joy. But I had to give up all my rights to follow Him. Luke 9:23 states, "And he said to all, 'If anyone would come after me, let him deny himself and take up his cross daily and follow me'" (ESV). When we try to hold onto our rights to be married, loved, accepted, healthy, or whatever we think we have a right to, we are only revealing our pride. Holding onto our rights sets us up for anger and bitterness. Often it is anger toward God. Please understand that I am not saying that if you give up your rights, you will definitely get what you desire. I can't promise that. Surrendering your rights to the Lord means trusting an all-powerful God to do His will in your life and allowing Him to align your desires with His desires.

When I surrendered, I knew God would not fail me and that He could hold my rights much better than I. In fact, He rejoiced over me, just like Isaiah 62:5 states. Had anyone ever rejoiced over me before? In other words, had anyone ever been filled with delight and joy when thinking about me? Had anyone considered my strong personality, looks, and imperfections . . . and smiled? I certainly thought no one had happy thoughts about me. God's rejoicing over me was a lot to consider. In fact, I could hardly wrap my brain around it. But I could imagine myself dressed fully in white while Jesus waited for me with open arms.

All that was required of me was to turn my life over to Him. Prior to my surrender and full repentance, there was a barrier to my communication with God. Even though I was a Christian, the fruit of the Holy Spirit was not seen consistently in my life since I had not learned to abide and fully trust in Him. John 15:4 states, "Abide in me, and I in you. As the branch cannot bear fruit by itself, unless it abides in the vine, neither can you, unless you abide in me" (ESV). I had to empty myself completely and be filled with His Holy Spirit.

My life changed pretty dramatically, as you will find out in my story. No longer did I want to live a mediocre Christian life, but I was sold out. Someone said to me, "What you believe about God determines how obedient you are to Him." I thought a lot about this statement. I was not turning back, so I asked God to take me and change me for His good pleasure. It is impossible for us to change ourselves. Only He can do it.

God's Word came alive, and I found contentment in Jesus. He became the One I went to when I was lonely in my singleness, and I found that Jesus knew my deepest longings. Many single people come home to an empty house and Lean Cuisine®, but I felt the presence of God. One of the passages that began to mean a lot to me was Matthew 25:1–13, the parable of the ten virgins. Five were ready to meet the bridegroom, Jesus, upon His appearance, and five were not. Only the five who were prepared made it to the wedding feast. Being obedient to God, with His help and grace, became my commitment. His law and Word are for our good and protection.

Prior to this turning point, my energy in life came from success in my career. I feel sick when I reflect back on how poorly I treated others in my quest for success. I'll never do that again. When you have been broken, you can look back and see that you could have been more compassionate, gentle, and merciful with others. Jesus is compassionate and merciful. I knew He had a lot of rough edges to sand down in my life, especially my desire for self-sufficiency. Success was where I found my self-worth. Now it's found in Jesus alone. Living for Him became my focus, and it is only accomplished by God's Holy Spirit living and working in me.

I heard a minister say that if you stop spending time with the Lord, you are heading for a fall. That has been my experience. A chair in my bedroom became my place of prayer and study every morning. For the first time in my life, I understood Mary, the sister of Martha and Lazarus.

Mary, a single woman as far as we know, had her priorities straight. When Jesus was around, she sat at His feet soaking in everything He taught. Culturally, this was probably not what she should be doing as a woman. Her sister, Martha, certainly understood culture. She was in the kitchen preparing food for all the guests while Mary listened to the words of Jesus with the men. How many times have I let my busyness distract me like Martha was distracted? In Luke 10, a frustrated Martha went to Jesus and told Him to make Mary help her. Martha must have been a close friend to think she could boss Jesus around! Jesus gently told her:

> Martha, Martha, you are worried and bothered about so many things; but only one thing is necessary, for Mary has chosen the good part, which shall not be taken away from her.
> —Luke 10:41–42

Mary chose what was important—sitting at the feet of Jesus. Whatever Jesus reveals to us when we are in His Word at His feet can't be taken from us.

We see Mary again at Jesus' feet after her brother Lazarus died. After her brother had been dead for four days, Jesus came to their village. It was His perfect timing so that God could be glorified. It wasn't Martha or even Mary's timing, and it certainly wasn't Lazarus's timing! Jesus was on no one else's timetable. Martha ran out to meet Jesus first when she heard that He was almost there. She faced Him and said, "Lord, if You had been here, my brother would not have died" (John 11:21). Jesus assured her that her brother would be raised from the dead. Martha misunderstood. She thought He meant at the end of time. She did confess, however, that she believed Jesus was the Messiah, God's Son. Then she went back to the house and told Mary that Jesus was asking for her. Mary immediately went to Jesus and "fell at His feet, saying to Him, 'Lord, if You had been here, my brother would not have died'" (v. 32). She was in tears, and so was Jesus. But, she said no more. He understood her pain because He felt it as well. When Jesus called Lazarus from the grave, Mary was a witness. She had full trust in her Savior.

We see Mary at the feet of Jesus yet again. John 12:1–8 is one of the most beautiful passages in Scripture. After Jesus raised Lazarus from the dead, the plotters who wanted to kill Him were hot on His trail. Mary came into the picture again:

> Jesus, therefore, six days before the Passover, came to Bethany where Lazarus was, whom Jesus had raised from the dead. So they made Him a supper there, and Martha was serving; but Lazarus was one of those reclining at the table with Him. Mary then took a pound of very costly perfume of pure nard, and anointed the feet of Jesus and wiped His feet with her hair; and the house was filled with the fragrance of the perfume. But Judas Iscariot, one of His disciples, who was intending to betray Him, said, "Why was this perfume not sold for three hundred denarii and given to poor people?" Now he said this, not because he was concerned about the poor, but because he was a thief, and as he had the money box, he used to pilfer what was put into it. Therefore Jesus said, "Let her alone, so that she may keep it for the day of My burial. For you always have the poor with you, but you do not always have Me."

Can't you see Mary totally breaking tradition again, causing a scene, all because she loved Jesus? He changed her life. He raised her brother from the dead. At His feet, she worshiped Him, pouring costly perfume and wiping His feet with her hair. Most likely, the men in the room were aghast, but Jesus accepted her sacrifice as a preparation for His foretold Crucifixion and burial. He saw her pure heart, and it pleased Him.

Mary knew Jesus personally. She discovered the "one thing" that was important—Jesus. As I spend more time with Jesus, He gives me a desire and longing to worship and serve Him. I surrender daily to His plan in obedience and lay my desires at His feet.

Obedience, worship, and loyalty to God go hand in hand. Have you ever asked yourself if you are loyal to God? Disobedience may bring immediate relief in a situation, but it brings consequences. Obedience is costly, and so is worship. You may lose your friends, family, home, and a number of other things, but following Jesus is worth it. The reward is great. I've had experience in both disobedience and obedience and definitely prefer the outcome of following Him.

All I knew after my transformation was that I couldn't get enough of Jesus. As a single woman, I finally stopped focusing on finding a man to marry and instead put my sights on seeking Jesus, my true Prince. There is another prince, however, that doesn't like it when we seek Jesus. He is the prince of darkness. Satan was not ready for me to have victory in my thoughts and actions.

CHAPTER 2

Interference from the Villain

In a good story, there is a protagonist—the good guy—and an antagonist—usually the bad guy. If you are a Marvel movies fan, you know exactly what I'm talking about. Or if you like to read novels, part of the drama is what takes place between the forces of good and evil.

While novels and movies may be fictitious, the Christian has an enemy that is very real. The villain's name is Satan, the father of lies, the prince of darkness, Beelzebub, accuser of the brethren, the devil, angel of the bottomless pit, god of this world, serpent of old, Lucifer, murderer, thief, tempter—need I name more? He comes to steal, kill, and destroy (John 10:10). Satan wants to do all these things to God's children. He certainly stole my childhood and early adult life, but praise God, I was freed from bondage.

It doesn't take long to get Satan's attention when you surrender to Jesus. The enemy doesn't like for a Christian to live victoriously. Satan wants to make our lives miserable, and he goes to extraordinary ends to do so. He is extremely patient and conniving. When I decided to live for Jesus after years of taking my life in my own hands, everything started out great. Better than ever. But before long, I didn't know what hit me. Forgiving others was one of many areas in my life that God turned around when I trusted Him fully. I forgave those who had injured me over the years and thought that was that. Knowing my weakness in this area, that's where the enemy attacked. Suddenly, I was struggling with forgiveness issues again, and I thought, *Haven't I already dealt with this? Didn't I already forgive those people? Why am I dwelling on this again?*

When Satan tempted Jesus in the wilderness, Jesus always spoke God's Word to combat him. The enemy can't stand against the truth of God's Word. Combating spiritual warfare and fear and renewing one's mind with God's Word all go together. The only way to renew or reprogram the mind is to fill it with truth and remind ourselves that the devil does not want us to have the mind of Christ. It is a daily battle for all of us to fight off the lies of Satan. He wants to discourage us, make us doubt, cause fear, and question God's love.

As I immersed myself in God's Word and put it into my heart and mind, I learned some strategies to defeat the devil. Several passages of Scripture became important to me in this endeavor. One such passage tells me exactly how I should be thinking. Philippians 4:8 states:

> Finally, brethren, whatever is true, whatever is honorable, whatever is right, whatever is pure, whatever is lovely, whatever is of good repute, if there is any excellence and if anything worthy of praise, dwell on these things.

If I'm thinking truth instead of the enemy's lies, I have a defense against doubts and falsehood.

So that I won't go back and rehash the past, I can take Isaiah 43:18 to heart: "Do not call to mind the former things, or ponder things of the past." There's an old saying, "Don't drag a dead horse through the desert." In other words, don't let the bad things of your past define your future. To "ponder" means to overthink, consider, or contemplate. God had a purpose in telling us not to live in our past failures. He has forgiven us. "As far as the east is from the west, so far has He removed our transgressions from us" (Psalm 103:12). He does not recall our sins. We are fully forgiven. Satan tries to tell us that God has not forgiven us, and he also doesn't want us to believe that we have forgiven others who have wronged us. Our actions in the present must come by living in the Spirit. A Spirit-filled life exhibits "love, joy, peace, patience, kindness, goodness, faithfulness, gentleness, self-control" (Galatians 5:22–23 ESV). When one chooses to follow Christ, God gives us the Holy Spirit. Having wholesome and truthful thoughts leads us to life and peace.

I began to make it a practice to think about the lovingkindness and faithfulness of God. Psalm 92:2 declares these attributes: "To declare Your lovingkindness in the morning and Your faithfulness by night." I thought about how He guides our steps: "For You are my rock and my fortress; for Your name's sake You will lead me and guide me" (Psalm 31:3) and "I am the LORD your God, who teaches you to profit, who leads you in the way you should go" (Isaiah 48:17).

God is a faithful and wise guide. He is trustworthy. How do I know if I'm trusting God with something instead of listening to the devil? I don't worry about the situation. I rely on God's peace that only He can offer.

To renew my mind concerning one of a woman's most common pastimes—worrying—I say out loud a variety of verses. "So do not worry about tomorrow; for tomorrow will care for itself. Each day has enough trouble of its own" (Matthew 6:34). "For God has not given us a spirit of timidity, but of power and love and discipline" (2 Timothy 1:7). "The steadfast of mind You will keep in perfect peace, because he trusts in You" (Isaiah 26:3). "For God is not a God of confusion but of peace" (1 Corinthians 14:33). "Peace I leave with you; My peace I give to you; not as the world gives do I give to you. Do not let your heart be troubled, nor let it be fearful" (John 14:27).

What you think, and what you allow Satan to make you believe, defines your views on rejection, suffering, injustice, self-image, addiction, and a number of other negative elements from your past or present. It is so much more peaceful, positive, and true to think about God—His wonderful attributes—and believe His view of you—how precious you are in His sight, how you were made in His image, how you've been set free from your past and are fully forgiven, and how you can lead others to find Jesus, too. When you get right down to it, it's not necessarily that "you are what you eat"; it's more likely "you are what you think." Scripture even agrees with this concept. Proverbs 23:7 states, "For as he thinks within himself, so he is."

I would be lying to you if I said I never struggle with dwelling on lies Satan puts into my head. You cannot imagine the fear I had in sharing my story and writing this book! Thoughts came to my mind like, *You have failed so much in your Christian walk. What makes you think anyone will even read your book?* I've heard it all from Satan. These verses became my strategy every time Satan's lies surfaced about this book: "Do not fear, for I am with you; do not anxiously look about you, for I am your God. I will strengthen you, surely I will help you, surely I will uphold you with My righteous right hand" (Isaiah 41:10); "Fear not, for you will not be put to shame; And do not feel humiliated, for you will not be disgraced; but you will forget the shame of your youth" (Isaiah 54:4); "Have I not commanded you? Be strong and courageous! Do not tremble or be dismayed, for the LORD your God is with you wherever you go" (Joshua 1:9); "I sought the LORD, and He answered me, and delivered me from all my fears" (Psalm 34:4). These are powerful verses to combat the enemy as he attempts to defeat us. Satan wants to make us believe that what God has for us is not better than we can imagine. Satan wants to derail us.

When God led the Israelites out of captivity in Egypt, He used Moses to do it. Moses carried out God's instructions, even though he was scared. Pharaoh opposed Moses. But, Moses was obedient to God's instructions, and God delivered the Israelites from the bondage of slavery in Egypt. Even though the Jewish nation had to experience the wilderness (God obviously had some things to teach them still—40 years' worth of lessons), they were delivered. They weren't delivered before they followed what God told them to do either. They had to fully trust God through His servant Moses before they escaped from bondage. Trust and obedience go before deliverance. A heart surrendered to God is the first step toward deliverance from the past, Satan, and our failures. God does not show us what's down the road, but He shows us His plan one step at a time.

There is a game I remember playing as a child. It is called "Blindfold." A blindfold is put on the eyes of a participant. Another person leads the "blinded" player through dark rooms, passageways, even outside. The longer the blindfolded person can trust his guide, the better. The winner is the one who trusts until the end of the game.

Sometimes God asks us to do something that doesn't make sense. Satan loves when this happens! He can cause us to doubt God and rationalize why we can't possibly obey. Instead of letting Satan have his way with us, we must: "Submit therefore to God. Resist the devil and he will flee from you" (James 4:7).

Joseph was a man who knew how to flee from doubt, anger, bitterness, temptation, and holding a grudge. His fascinating story unfolds in Genesis. Jacob, whose favorite wife was Rachel, had a favorite son as well. That would be Joseph, one of Jacob's two sons with Rachel. Ten of Joseph's brothers were jealous of him. Joseph received a special coat from his father, he had dreams of ruling over his brothers, and he had his father's attention. His brothers seethed in anger, bitterness, and jealousy; they plotted their revenge. Finally, they threw him in a pit and sold him to traders traveling to Egypt. They covered up what they had done by lying to their father, saying that Joseph had been killed by a wild animal, and handing him Joseph's bloody coat to "prove" it.

Joseph ended up as a slave of Potiphar, Pharaoh's officer, in Egypt. He had a lot of time to think about why his brothers hated him so much. I'm sure he did some real soul searching. God was with Joseph, so whatever Joseph did in Egypt was successful (Genesis 39:2–3). He was trusted by Potiphar and was made overseer of Potiphar's household. Everyone loved Joseph. But soon, he started to get the attention of Potiphar's wife, and she "looked with desire at Joseph" (v. 7). To make a long story short,

Joseph resisted her advances, was falsely accused, ended up in jail, correctly interpreted some dreams, got out of jail, and was made Pharaoh's right-hand man.

Joseph prepared the kingdom for a coming drought by storing up grain. Eventually, his brothers were sent by their father to buy grain, and they made their way unknowingly to the brother they sold into slavery. When Joseph recognized his brothers, he was overcome with emotion. Instead of loathing them and seeking revenge, he forgave his brothers and wept with love for them.

> But Joseph said to them, "Do not be afraid, for am I in God's place? As for you, you meant evil against me, but God meant it for good in order to bring about this present result, to preserve many people alive." —Genesis 50:19–20

I can relate to Joseph. Joseph dealt with alienation, rejection, and injustice. He was falsely accused and lied about. He had to persevere when he saw no end in sight. His hope was in God, his Redeemer and Restorer. He chose to love and forgive and not be in bondage to bitterness and unforgiveness. God used many specific verses throughout my life to help me know His truth and deliverance from anger and bitterness. Once I chose to forgive and keep forgiving, Satan could not have power over me.

I am reminded of Anne Graham Lotz's view on forgiveness in her book, *The Joy of My Heart*. She said:

> We forgive others, not because they deserve it, *but because He deserves it!* The only reason we have to forgive is that He commands us to, and our obedience gives us opportunity to say to Him, "Thank You for forgiving me. I love You." Our forgiveness of others then becomes an act of worship that we would not enter into except for who He is and for the overwhelming debt of love we owe Him.

Forgiving one another is an act of worship! This concept had not occurred to me before. And Satan did not want me to believe this truth.

We are commanded in 1 Peter 5:8 to watch out for Satan. "Be of sober spirit, be on the alert. Your adversary, the devil, prowls around like a roaring lion, seeking someone to devour." We are also commanded to root out certain things in our lives.

> Do not grieve the Holy Spirit of God, by whom you were sealed for the day of redemption. Let all bitterness and wrath and anger and clamor and slander be put away from you, along with all malice. Be kind to one another, tender-hearted, forgiving each other, just as God in Christ also has forgiven you.
> —Ephesians 4:30–32

Jesus Christ defeats Satan—past, present, and future. And so can we. Single women deal with some issues that married women may or may not. I want to mention a few ways that Satan can destroy the lives of single, Christian women. Here are some bold-faced lies that Satan whispers and Scripture to throw back at him:

Lie:
"Go ahead and sleep with him. It's OK. This is the twenty-first century."

Truth:
"Marriage is to be held in honor among all, and the marriage bed is to be undefiled; for fornicators and adulterers God will judge" (Hebrews 13:4).

Lie:
"You can't stay single. Marry the first person who takes an interest in you, even if he doesn't meet your high standards and you have doubts, because you can change him after you're married. There's no need to wait."

Truth:
"For from days of old they have not heard or perceived by ear, nor has the eye seen a God besides You, who acts in behalf of the one who waits for Him" (Isaiah 64:4).

Lie:

"Climb all over people as you push up the career ladder. You deserve it."

Truth:

"You shall love your neighbor as yourself" (Matthew 22:39).

Lie:

"Nobody cares about you. Nobody loves you."

Truth:

"For God so loved the world, that He gave His only begotten Son, that whoever believes in Him shall not perish, but have eternal life" (John 3:16).

Lie:

"You're not pretty, thin, pure, or attractive enough to get a man who follows the ways of God."

Truth:

"For God sees not as man sees, for man looks at the outward appearance, but the LORD looks at the heart" (1 Samuel 16:7).

Lie:

"People will always leave you. You are alone."

Truth:

"Be strong and courageous, do not be afraid or tremble at them, for the LORD your God is the one who goes with you. He will not fail you or forsake you" (Deuteronomy 31:6).

Lie:

"It doesn't matter if I am a Christian and my fiancé (or boyfriend) is not. He will become a Christian after we are married."

Truth:

"Do not be unequally yoked with unbelievers. For what partnership has righteousness with lawlessness? Or what fellowship has light with darkness?" (2 Corinthians 6:14 ESV).

I understand what it means to fight the enemy with Scripture. My thoughts can really be messed up when I don't rely on God's Word. I can only renew my mind with God's Word. It's not a one-time event. Every day we have to renew our minds through prayer and by spending time in the Bible. I often think of illustrations from the medical profession because I'm a physician assistant (PA). Germs are invisible. They are microorganisms that, given the right conditions, can cause disease. Bad germs can zap a body's nutrients and energy and can produce toxins. They can spread, and before you know it, they take control. Germs are in the air, on our bodies, on surfaces—you name it, a germ is there. The way we fight against harmful germs is through good hygiene and building up our defenses with good health. It doesn't take a brain surgeon to understand how this illustration relates to Satan's lies.

Ephesians 6:11–13 instructs us to:

> Put on the full armor of God, so that you will be able to stand firm against the schemes of the devil. For our struggle is not against flesh and blood, but against the rulers, against the powers, against the world forces of this darkness, against the spiritual forces of wickedness in the heavenly places. Therefore, take up the full armor of God, so that you will be able to resist in the evil day, and having done everything, to stand firm.

Read the next few verses of Ephesians 6, and you will find specific pieces of armor that have intended purposes in fighting the enemy.

When I finally surrendered my life completely to Christ, I was done allowing Satan's deceptions to destroy me and my future. I believed God when He said in Jeremiah 29:11 that He would give me "a future and a hope." I realized God truly loved me, and He was enough. I really didn't have to be married to find joy—I certainly didn't want to settle for anything less than God's will. Satan will tempt you with anything you think you must have other than God to make you happy. But profound joy only comes by knowing and following the Prince of Peace.

Broken and redeemed both describe my life. For a long time, I believed Satan and thought no one else felt as insecure, lonely, and rejected as I did. These are real feelings among women, even Christian women, whether single or married. No matter what your story, there is hope. Jesus is our only hope, and "He drew me up from the pit of destruction, out of the miry bog, and set my feet upon a rock, making my steps secure" (Psalm 40:2 ESV). Jesus became my strong rock, my fortress of defense against the enemy. But I did not give Jesus preeminence as a way of life until I was nearly 50. I did for short periods, but it didn't fully click until I gave Him everything.

CHAPTER 3

Acquainted with the Ashes

Happy birthday to me. A few friends in my hometown of Charlotte, North Carolina, invited me over to celebrate my fiftieth birthday, but I didn't want to make a big deal over the milestone. Turning 40 was a totally different story. I panicked. It was a big deal that I was not exactly living the life I had imagined. Turning 50, I had, for the most part, accepted a life of being single but with a determination to make the best of it. As you will learn, my experiences and circumstances before age 50 brought me to the end of my rope. Jesus was the One to reach down and rescue me.

I wasn't a "loner" and certainly did not isolate myself from men, but I no longer focused on one day meeting Prince Charming who would carry me over the threshold of matrimony. I finally had a life dedicated to Jesus and was essentially undistracted by men because I started to concentrate on things that mattered rather than on being accepted by men and getting a date. It was freeing.

Admittedly, it did take a while to accept the fact that I probably would never be married and that I would live life alone. I used to put God in a box and give Him a time line for nuptials between my future prince and me because, let's face it, the "Barbie" image had messed with the mind of this single woman. The tall, skinny, and fashionable stereotype puts girls like me to shame. But, I couldn't get enough of her when I was growing up. I imagined my chubby self blossoming into an attractive woman one day, and I spent hours looking through department store catalogs, cutting out pictures of beautiful models, and making up stories that they had perfect marriages and lots of kids.

I wanted to look like Barbie, as did most little girls like me who grew up in the 60s and 70s. However, Cinderella seemed more relatable to me. Cinderella represented a kind, young woman who was alone in the world, ill-treated, had a propensity for talking to herself or mice, when, out of nowhere, a fairy godmother changed her life and made it possible for her to meet her future husband. She gave me hope, since I too felt like an unloved orphan who dreamed of being the choice of a prince. However, while storybook fantasies and dolls remained in the back of my mind, I placed God in a self-created box concerning my own happily-ever-after, which limited His bigness and did a number on my contentment. To free Him from my parameters, God had something to prove to me. Why did it take me so long to realize that I could not treat Him like He was my fairy godmother? It took years to learn that He is Holy God who is worthy to be worshiped, honored, and obeyed.

As I looked at my singleness at age 50, my three biggest realities were: I was alone, I would have to support myself now and in the future, and I would grow old without companionship or someone to love and take care of me if I no longer could. These realities scared me to death for many years, especially because I had no living relatives who played a major role in my life. Yet, because of my forced independence from a young age, I felt it was up to me to take my "negatives" and turn them into positives.

The positive thing about being alone is that a person has some freedoms. No one tells you what to do or how to manage your life. I can't tell you how many times married women would comment on how envious they were that I could come and go as I pleased, make my own decisions, and be adventurous. Singleness definitely is free from many family constraints and, at times, especially observing friends with children, I counted my blessings.

I tried not to hang around singles only, because that is a warped sense of the real world. I avoided singles' social events and clubs. I instead socialized with families, couples, and married women so that I was included into society. Frankly, being accepted was the driving force in my life for a long time—until I truly understood that God accepts me as I am. Loneliness and rejection are partners that consume a single's life, if allowed. And at half a century, my goal was to not get sucked up into the negative implications of that major reality. I had lived much of my life feeling lonely and rejected. My heart longed to give my love to someone, and I had prayed that God would allow this desire to be fulfilled. I often tried to escape overwhelming feelings of loneliness by shopping. I was never satisfied or happy with myself no matter what clothes, makeup, or hairstyle I tried. Even when I lost enough weight to fit in a size six, I still was not happy or truly content. I thought if I could change my appearance, it would result in contentment and self-confidence.

For the most part, I was good at providing for myself as a PA. I was not a beauty queen, so I concentrated on my intellect. On my fiftieth birthday, I didn't have a husband's retirement income to fall back on, so I did what I could to insure that I wouldn't rely on the government to support me one day. Having a successful career was my financial security. It allowed me to be independent, but it also made me somewhat intimidating to others, especially men. An emergency room doctor friend once told me, "You know, Claude, I probably couldn't handle dating you. You just really intimidate men." Not knowing what he meant, I encouraged him to tell me why. He continued, in a jovial manner, "You are so confident, self-assured, and smart. Men want to be needed. You don't need a man." I was surprised, but the more I thought about what he said, I realized that my confidence wasn't in myself anymore, it was in Jesus. He had taken my insecurities and had made me secure. Jesus completed me.

For as much as I benefited from Jesus completing me and also having a good career, the hardest reality was to have a positive outlook regarding not being married. Trusting God with this reality became a test of surrendering everything to Him. This turn of my will to complete surrender took years, with a lot of life happening before coming to the end of myself. Fear is the result of a fixation on being by oneself or being rejected, and I was an expert on its byproducts—anxiety, depression, and impatience.

Scripture like 1 Peter 5:7 eventually became my motto, "casting all your anxiety on Him, because He cares for you," along with Psalm 37:8, "Do not fret; it leads only to evildoing." The Lord showed me that the alternative to worry and fear was in the previous verses: "Commit your way to the LORD, trust also in Him, and He will do it . . . Rest in the LORD and wait patiently for Him" (Psalm 37:5, 7). Everything rests on trusting Him patiently. He always does what is best for us, even if we don't understand His ways. By trusting in His plan instead of my own, and praising Him for it instead of grumbling, even when the total picture isn't clear yet, I can then understand Psalm 62:5: "My soul, wait in silence for God only, for my hope is from Him."

At a crossroad in my life, more than anything, I didn't want others to pity me for still being single. I didn't want to be invited places because "poor Claudia has nowhere else to go," but I wanted to be with people who accepted me as a friend. Because that's what I exuded, for the most part, that's how people treated me. God knows what we need before we ask (Matthew 6:8), and I could trust Him for my friends, my security, and my needs. When I didn't have a date to events, I began to see God as described in Isaiah 54:5—"For your husband is your Maker, whose name is the LORD of hosts; and your Redeemer is the Holy One of Israel, who is called the God of all the earth."

My generation grew up watching shows like *Leave It To Beaver*, *The Brady Bunch*, and *My Three Sons*, through which singles of all ages unknowingly accepted the concept of an ideal marriageable age, whatever that age is. Modern television programs still present unrealistic "norms" in many respects. To live under the banner of "single" can sometimes be exhausting, especially if you aren't content being single. One thing I know—which became more important to me as I aged—living a life conformed to the image of Christ is actually possible when I am content. Scripture is clear on this point.

> But godliness *actually* is a means of great gain when accompanied by contentment. For we have brought nothing into the world, so we cannot take anything out of it either.
> —1 Timothy 6:6–7, author's emphasis

Being satisfied with my circumstances not only brought gain but truly helped others be content with the fact that I was single as well. Really, one can only take so many blind dates or remarks about "setting you up." Trying to attract the opposite sex can be downright taxing on a person's time and so can listening to others who want to play matchmaker, oblivious to the fact that they may be contributing to a single woman's temptation to be discontent. Is it possible to learn "to be content in whatever circumstances I am" as Paul states in Philippians 4:11? I think so, or his statement would not be found in God's Word.

It took a long time to get to the point of Jesus being the One to lean on and be satisfied with, believe me. A childhood perception of not being good enough and other bumps along the road to contentment contributed to a pattern of insecurity and self-rejection that only my Creator could erase over time. God has answers for rejection, injustice, victimization, fear, brokenness, loneliness, and Satan's lies concerning who you are. God's answers are found in His Word, and at times, through the testimonies of His people who have walked in the same shoes. Let's just say I've walked some miles in my life.

David Platt, in his book, *Counter Culture*, makes an interesting statement that I believe applies to anything that tries to arrest our attention from devotion to God, "For in all our running to serve ourselves, we're actually rebelling against the only One who can satisfy our souls." Focusing on finding a mate, having a successful career, being accepted, or seeking to be beautiful or rich can compete with following Jesus.

There was a time that I sought everything but Jesus. When do the lies of what will make us happy come? Early on, there's no doubt. We are inundated with it from parents' expectations and opinions, movies, books, social media, and culture. It took a while for me to understand, particularly on the topic of singleness, that it's OK to be married or single as long as that is God's plan for one who follows Him with an undivided heart. Being focused on Jesus is far more important than your marital state.

Isn't it interesting how much our childhood shapes our thoughts and actions? That's when my predefined and unrealistic "happily ever after" began to mock me. My life started in the cinders rather than the palace ball, but was it possible for a prince to choose me? My story is one of learning the hard way to be content in all circumstances, because Jesus wants my life to be a reflection of Him whether single, married, successful in a career, jobless, a mother, without children, wealthy, poor, attractive, unattractive, or whatever.

It's time to tell you my testimony of God's grace. I pray it will give hope to anyone who needs an honest account of someone who got some things right and more things wrong as a single woman for 54 years and now as a happily married woman. It is a love story between a scarred woman and the Prince of Peace who rescued me from myself. Jesus, our Redeemer, gives "a garland instead ashes . . . praise instead of a spirit of fainting . . . So they will be called oaks of righteousness, the planting of the LORD, that He may be glorified" (Isaiah 61:3).

CHAPTER 4

Building Walls of Self-Protection

One of my favorite movies is *The Mirror Has Two Faces*, a 1996 film featuring Barbara Streisand and Jeff Bridges. Basically, the plot is about an English professor at Columbia University who is single, not very pretty, smart, and, sadly, lives with her domineering and beautiful mother. If I looked in a mirror, this character would be me at one time in my life. She ends up attracting the attention of a character, played by Bridges, who wants to marry someone who will agree to a platonic relationship only. However, after they are married, Streisand's character actually falls in love with her husband and strategizes to make him fall in love with her. She diets, exercises, and transforms into someone she thinks will get his attention.

Ridiculous, I know. The characters actually do appear to end up with a happy and fulfilled marriage. I used to watch that movie over and over again thinking, *If she can find someone, I can too!* I had a lot of issues to work through, not only from my childhood but from my own image of myself that I had created as a defense mechanism.

It took a while for me to see the protective walls I had built up around myself over years of rejection, even if at times the rebuff was only perceived. Feeling unloved and unaccepted made me isolate myself. I wanted someone to love me, but my heart, in my mind, was damaged enough by people. My goal became to protect my heart, even if it meant living life alone. I could handle no more rejection. Someone said to me once, "Claudia, I am afraid that the walls you put up to keep from risking hurt may never go down. In fact, I think you might not know how to get them down even now." What I viewed as rejection formed me into a young adult who didn't understand God's unconditional love. And it took many years before the walls were destroyed.

I grew up as the older of two children to parents who did not know how to adequately express unconditional love. I am absolutely positive that they did love me immensely, but neither knew how to say the words or show affection to a little girl who needed a hug and words of affirmation.

My mother was beautiful. She occasionally modeled clothing for a retail store's advertisements in our local newspaper, and truly she was the loveliest woman I knew. She had a perfect figure and could eat anything without gaining a pound. It's possible that she would have even been pretty dressed in a potato sack. She was constantly complimented, although she did not feel beautiful. I wanted to look like her and have her poise and grace. In her high school years, she was the homecoming queen and known as the local beauty. I, on the other hand, was overweight, awkward, and the opposite of my mother in appearance and personality.

My father was not affectionate or attentive as many dads are today, but honestly, I think most men of his generation could fit into that category. He provided well for his family. He came home tired from work and rarely ate dinner with us. Actually, our family only ate together on Sundays after church when Mom made her delicious roast and mashed potatoes. My dad and I connected well when we talked about spiritual things. Since he was a Sunday School teacher, we often discussed the lesson he was working on, even when I was a child, and I loved hearing his calm and soothing voice tell me about the things of God. He taught me a lot about God through his quiet example and wisdom. He was never critical of me. When I was in college and had a problem or was upset, my father was the first person I called. He was wise and always knew what to say. I'm not sure I ever heard him say that he loved me though. I'm not sure he knew how to say those words, which could have been a generational thing.

My parents' marriage was good, I think. They were committed to one another. My father had the patience of Job with my mom, who could be more than a little controlling. I'm sure that her own childhood formed her personality, and perhaps she had not dealt with her own insecurities and pain. Unfortunately, I perceived that I was never good enough for my mother since I wasn't pretty and thin. I did not meet society's definition of beautiful. There were times I thought she was ashamed of me.

I developed a low self-image. At the end of the day, I own the responsibility for this view of myself, although my circumstances certainly helped shape my perceptions. I often felt rejected by my mother and peers in school, but ultimately my response to my circumstances created huge cement blocks that were the foundation of a protective fortress I constructed around myself. Self-doubt, self-pity, and self-loathing became the filters of my life, even while in elementary school. One of the nicknames other children called me was "Lumpy." So I kept to my studies and myself and isolated from potential friends. It was too hard to make a friend and wasn't worth the effort. My mom didn't reach out or welcome any acquaintances of mine while I was growing up until my college roommate. I'm not sure why, but I often felt guilty for having fun when I was younger.

At age nine, I professed Christ as my Savior. I understood parts of the gospel, but a personal relationship with Him was not something I grasped. At that point in my life, I had not figured out God accepted and loved me for who I was and wanted me to talk to Him about my heartaches as well as my dreams. I was too accustomed to rejection and disappointing others, so it was hard not to transfer that into how I thought God viewed me. I thought that I had to earn God's approval and love.

I sought counseling many years after my childhood. The counselor asked me if I knew the song, "Jesus Loves Me." I told him I did, and he asked me to say the words. He said I believed the words only because the Bible said it, but I did not believe it in my heart. He was right. I had asked God numerous times why He even chose to create me. Since I thought people rejected me, I thought God must reject me, although nothing could have been further from the truth.

One way I coped with rejection was through food. Some people get a hobby, some people become alcoholics, but I ate like nobody's business. The more I consumed, the more weight I gained. I used to hate to see a photo of myself. I ate to soothe the ache in my heart every day after school. I was a "latchkey kid," so I was lonely both at school and at home. When girls in my neighborhood asked me to spend the night, I refused. It wasn't that I did not want to go, but it was scary to think I could not go to the kitchen and eat if I felt insecure, something I did at home a lot when I compared myself to my mother. In my mind, I just did not fit in anywhere—at home or at school. I constantly asked myself, "What is wrong with me?" I felt shame as a child because I did not believe that I measured up.

For the most part, in high school, I was invisible. I liked it that way. I didn't have a boyfriend or any significant girlfriends, so I put all my energy into making high grades. At least that was something I was good at and a place I could get a feeling of satisfaction and self-worth. In the seventh grade, there was a boy I liked; I wanted his attention. One day, I received a folded note from another girl. When I opened it, I was thrilled! It was from that boy! Inside it said that he liked me and had his initials. Wow! He really liked me! Before the class was over, however, he found out about the note, which he had not written, and immediately told me that he could never care for me. A "friend" of mine thought it would be funny to play a joke on me. It was cruel. I could not get the rejection out of my mind. I cried so hard when I got home.

When it was time to go to college, I believed there was no way that I would attend anything but a girls' school, so I applied to an all-girls college, which was only a couple of hours north from my hometown of Charlotte. I thought that I would be safe with girls. There were no sororities, so I wouldn't be excluded. I wouldn't be rejected by a guy on campus because there were no guys, and I wouldn't have to worry about trying to be beautiful, perfect, or accepted by males. What saved me in college was my roommate. She was a breath of fresh air—positive, spiritual, and happy. She made me laugh and accepted me for me. Praise and affirmation for me came out of her mouth all the time, and I began to think perhaps I was worth something. She was the Energizer bunny of encouragement, and after a while, I even began to believe a few positive things about myself. It's amazing what a word of affirmation can do for a person. Interestingly, while I made some positive changes those first years of college, I still could not see them as positive. The mirror only told me that I was still an ugly girl that no one wanted.

At one point in college, our school announced a formal in which we had to ask a guy to come as our date. I wasn't going to attend the dance until my roommate insisted. There was a young man from another school who caught my eye, but I thought he wouldn't come with me. I first noticed him when he attended a class on our campus. He was cute and many girls would have given anything to date him, even my roommate. I finally got up enough courage to ask him, and he accepted. I was so happy and excited. I couldn't believe it. It would be my first dance; I had not gone to my high school prom. We had a good time at the dance, and he actually started returning my interest. But as soon as that happened, I added a few more blocks to the fortress that surrounded me by deciding to not return his interest. There was too much potential for getting hurt, and there was no way I would risk being rejected. He really scared me. How could he possibly be interested in me? I didn't fit the criteria of being pretty enough to have a boyfriend, or so I convinced myself. I decided not to date the incredible young man, because the risk of being rejected was too much to bear. I wrote him a letter saying that although I really liked him, it would be best if we didn't pursue a relationship. That set me on a course to protect my heart and avoid men. I didn't date. My self-worth became focused on my studies and my future career.

I was given an opportunity to study abroad at Oxford University for a summer while in college. That meant that I would graduate earlier, in

December instead of the following May. I was somewhat concerned about leaving my dad, since he was having some health issues, but everything seemed to fall into place to go to England with my college roommate and other friends . . . until my mother stepped in two weeks before my departure and adamantly forbade me to go. I was devastated. My opportunity to travel, to see the world, was taken from me, and I resented it. When the plane left for England without me, I cried. Years later, my dad told me that my mom was afraid for me to go overseas, fearing that she would lose me. Because I was not walking closely with the Lord at that time in my life, blocks of resentment were stacked in my heart, adding to the blocks of rejection and self-loathing. I created quite a wall!

Studying biology and chemistry, I set my attention on getting into medical school. I wanted to be a doctor. I knew if I could be a doctor, I might be good enough in the eyes of others and live up to my own aspirations. I would have the self-worth that I sought. Although I graduated with honors, received recommendations from my professors, and my interviews were good, my scores were not as high as I anticipated on the MCAT, the standardized test to get into medical school. My father, who was on the parents' board for my college and had spoken to the president of the school, called me to say that the president told him I would be accepted into a medical school in North Carolina. Finally, the letter arrived. I was shaking when I opened it and read these words, "We regret to inform you . . ." Rejected rather than accepted! This rejection wasn't supposed to happen! My father was just as surprised as I was. With my dreams dashed, I fell on the floor of my dorm room and bawled.

My biology professor encouraged me to apply to the PA program at Duke University. Before I could apply, Duke required that an applicant complete 2,000 hours of direct patient contact. I volunteered time at nursing homes and an emergency room—anything to get patient contact hours. I was accepted at Duke in 1982, and for two years I worked and studied to get my degree. My second year in the program, I did a rotation in internal medicine at Duke University Hospital, and things were looking up. I thoroughly loved Duke and made a lot of friends. When I graduated as a PA,

I was certified in both surgery and primary care with high scores on the standardized tests in those areas. There was no doubt that I felt vindicated for doing so well since I failed to get into medical school.

Throughout college and graduate school, I went to church and had a semblance of spirituality. I observed a daily "quiet time" with the Lord and sought God for His direction, but I wasn't growing spiritually or living a consistent Spirit-filled life. I was not characterized by a spirit of thanksgiving. The Fruit of the Spirit, as listed in Galatians 5:22–23, was not evident in my life on a regular basis. I did not live in complete submission to God. Because of the time I spent in the Bible, however, the Lord began to reveal to me that my own pride and fear kept me from the healing that I desperately needed. There was no doubt that I had a warped sense of what it took to redeem me from my self-destructive view of myself and others. But instead of surrendering all of my pain to Him, my answer to the rejection I had experienced was to become more and more self-reliant. Creating a false sense of security in my mind, I continued to build up massive walls of self-preservation. And that was my problem. Self-focus takes on many shapes. It doesn't have to be about appearance at all. It can be on anything that promotes or preserves self. On this, I was an expert.

Although it was years before I realized what went wrong, only Jesus could save me from myself. I needed the Prince of Peace more than anything.

CHAPTER 5

When Wrong Thinking Takes Root

Discontentment in marriage caused a lot of problems in biblical times. Fortunately not all marriages mentioned in the Bible portray circumstances in which deceit, bitterness, or jealousy complicated relationships, or there would have been more like Paul who encouraged us to remain single like he was (1 Corinthians 7:8)! Case in point, the story of Jacob and his marital dysfunction. I'm really not sure what possessed (or possesses) men to have more than one wife. It's not ever going to be pretty because it's not God's design (Genesis 2:15–25). Marriage is designed to be a picture of Christ's relationship with His bride, the Church (Ephesians 5:23–27). Besides, women are just not wired to share the roost with another woman!

Of all the tragic women in the Bible, I think Leah tops the list. When most people read the story of Jacob, they tend to feel sorry for him. The morning after his wedding, Jacob realizes that he married Leah instead of her younger sister, Rachel, who is his one true love. Or they feel sorry for

Rachel because she is denied a wedding that was promised to her. These are valid opinions. There definitely was some underhandedness perpetrated by Jacob's Uncle Laban, Leah and Rachel's father.

Leah, however, has my pity. The woman was a victim of a lifelong propensity for rejection. The eldest daughter of Laban, Jacob's mother's brother, she was not the pretty sister or the favorite—that was Rachel. I'm sure Leah would not have been homecoming queen. Jacob was sent by his father, Isaac, to Paddan-aram to Uncle Laban's house in order to marry one of his cousins (Genesis 28). When he arrived in his uncle's homeland, Jacob saw a well where men had gathered their flocks of sheep (Genesis 29). He asked the men if they knew Laban, which they did, and they looked around to point out Laban's daughter, Rachel, who was coming toward the well with her father's sheep. It was love at first sight. Jacob quickly moved the stone that covered the well and proceeded to water the sheep that Rachel shepherded. He greeted her with a kiss and introduced himself as her cousin. Rachel ran home to tell her father, who immediately walked to meet his nephew and welcome Jacob to their home.

For the next month, Jacob made himself at home and helped out with the chores. In that time, knowing he came for the purpose of finding a wife, he took a good look at his two female cousins. The Bible tells us that Leah had some sort of problem with her eyes, so perhaps she squinted all the time, was cross-eyed, or had an eye disease. We don't know. Rachel, on the other hand, was "beautiful in form and appearance" (Genesis 29:17 ESV), translated into today's terms as "hot." When Laban asked Jacob how he could repay him for the work he had done, Jacob was ready with an answer and put Plan A into action. He was in love with Rachel, so he told Laban that he would work for him for seven years if he could have Rachel as his wife.

But after the seven years of Jacob's hard labor, Leah was still single. Laban didn't want the younger daughter to marry before the older. So Laban tricked Jacob and somehow substituted Leah for Rachel on the wedding night (Genesis 29:21–23). Oh, my goodness! Whatever on earth possessed Leah to go along with her father's plan, I'll never know. Maybe she truly hated her sister, or maybe her father didn't give her a choice. And did Laban tie Rachel up somewhere during the wedding ceremony and put a sock in her mouth? Who knows! The morning after their union, Jacob woke up to Leah. Immediately Jacob rushed out of the tent to find Laban and said, "What is this you have done to me? Was it not for Rachel that I served with you? Why then have you deceived me?" (Genesis 29:25). Can you imagine the pain Leah felt when she saw the surprise and disgust in Jacob's eyes the next morning and then heard him yell at her father that she wasn't in the bargain?

It's a complicated, true story of sibling rivalry, unrequited love, lies, and jealousy. For Leah, this was most likely one more rejection to add to her life-time of being disregarded by available men in the area. She wasn't wanted when her identity was first revealed to Jacob, and she never became wanted by her husband. Upon delivering her firstborn, Reuben, she said, "Because the LORD has looked upon my affliction; for now my husband will love me" (Genesis 29:32 ESV). But having a child didn't change things because at the birth of her second son, she said, "Because the LORD has heard that I am hated, he has given me this son also" (Genesis 29:33 ESV). Not even a second son got Jacob's attention. When her third son was born, she still felt slighted. She said, "Now this time my husband will be attached to me, because I have borne him three sons" (Genesis 29:34 ESV). But even four sons did not cause Jacob to love his first wife or her sons more than Rachel and her two sons, Joseph and Benjamin. As a result, Leah allowed the roots of bitterness to seep into fertile soil made ready and tilled by rejection and mistreatment from others, even though God showed her compassion by giving her sons. Her sadness at being mistreated was not sin. But when she allowed anger and bitterness to take root in her heart, Leah sinned.

Bitterness, jealousy, covetousness, self-pity, and a host of other sins are born out of wrong thinking. Notice that I didn't say rejection. The rejection I felt during my childhood and early adulthood wasn't sin, but my sinful response to it was. I developed a critical and judgmental spirit regarding others and myself. I used those judgments of others to somehow feel better about myself. However, only Jesus has the authority to judge man's motives and actions (John 5:22). I was jealous of those who were married, and felt I had the "right" to be married. This was pride, pure and simple. I strove for perfection within myself and for others. *Grace* was not in my vocabulary. It took time for me to forgive any offense. My self-loathing and inability to forgive created jealousy, bitterness, and self-centeredness. It was all about me. In James 3:16, the Bible states, "For where jealousy and selfish ambition exist, there will be disorder and every vile practice" (ESV).

I did not like my life or myself, but I did not know how to change. All of my self-worth was tied up in my accomplishments. My appearance and my self-sufficiency had become my idols. By calling myself a Christian without acting like one, I was deeply grieving the Holy Spirit. I grew to learn that I was denying my Savior, Jesus Christ, in my life. Ephesians 4:30 states, "And do not grieve the Holy Spirit of God, by whom you were sealed for the day of redemption" (ESV). It took me a long time to learn that God had a plan for my life, and He was entirely trustworthy to work things out for my good.

I totally get where Leah was coming from. She did not measure up to her sister's beauty and, in my mind, I couldn't compare to my mother or other girls. Other girls were beautiful and thin, while I was overweight and felt ugly. I believed that I was a disappointment to others, especially my mom. Many nights I cried myself to sleep and then got up in the middle of the night to ravage the refrigerator for comfort. Laban certainly didn't think Leah's prospects for a husband were good, which I'm sure made Leah feel like she couldn't compare to her little sister. In fact, her father actually used her to get more years of service from Jacob.

There's no doubt Leah had self-worth issues from living in a dysfunctional family. My perception was that only pretty girls with good figures were worthy to be loved and cherished, and I imagine Leah felt the same way. Although my father encouraged me and accepted me by his actions, saying, "I love you," holding me, or taking me anywhere with him were not his ways. The only time I remember him playing with me or my sibling was when we were on vacation at the beach. So I created a scenario in my mind: I was not pretty enough to be loved and accepted by either of my parents. I didn't realize at the time that this thought was a lie from the enemy, Satan.

Years after my father's death, at the time of my mother's passing, I stood in the receiving line at her funeral. A friend of my father greeted me and said, "Did you know that you were the apple of your dad's eye? He loved you so much!" I broke into tears. God sent that man to assure me that my father had loved me, and the peace and relief I felt comforted me completely.

The lies of Satan are very convincing. He attempts to destroy lives. I was not acquainted with tactical spiritual warfare during the formative years of my life. I may have known some of the truth about Satan from Sunday School, but the truth had not been transferred from my brain to my heart. I had not had an "aha" moment yet in my Christian life. Although others assured me repeatedly that my identity could be found completely in Jesus Christ instead of my own feelings of insecurity, the truth of this concept had not taken root. Much later I would fully grasp, "and you will know the truth, and the truth will set you free" (John 8:32 ESV).

I remember having a conversation with my pastor when I was ten. I don't recall what started the conversation, but I do remember telling him that I wasn't happy. When he asked why, I said, "If I enjoy myself, something bad will happen." Even though he tried to tell me that what I believed was not God's plan and was not true, this lie was deeply rooted.

As for Leah and for me, if we had believed God early on and known our self-worth was only in Him, we would have been spared much misery. His Word is clear for the one who feels rejected. If I ever doubt His love and care for me, I need only to meditate on Psalm 139:13–18. From the moment of my conception, God loved me, formed me, and knew me:

> For You formed my inward parts; You wove me in my mother's womb. I will give thanks to You, for I am fearfully and wonderfully made; wonderful are Your works, and my soul knows it very well. My frame was not hidden from You, when I was made in secret, and skillfully wrought in the depths of the earth; Your eyes have seen my unformed substance; and in Your book were all written the days that were ordained for me,

> when as yet there was not one of them. How precious also are
> Your thoughts to me, O God! How vast is the sum of them! If I
> should count them, they would outnumber the sand.

God understands us better than anyone. He made me wonderfully for a purpose. Does He think that I'm not good enough, pretty enough, or thin enough? Absolutely not! His thoughts toward me are precious. That is an awesome revelation if it is fully grasped. In Isaiah 43:4 we hear the Lord say, "you are precious in My sight," and, "I love you." He is so acquainted with us that "the very hairs of your head are all numbered" (Matthew 10:30).

Why should we believe that God actually understands our feelings of rejection? Because Jesus Himself was rejected. Isaiah 53:3 reminds me that "He was despised and forsaken of men, a man of sorrows and acquainted with grief; and like one from whom men hide their face He was despised, and we did not esteem Him." When I experience trauma or difficulty, I'm much more willing to receive comfort and a listening ear from someone who has experienced a similar situation. Jesus understands rejection. He was not accepted as the Messiah in His own hometown (Mark 6:1–5). He was crucified at the hands of His own people. Despite how we may picture Him, Isaiah 53:2 does not portray the movie version of Jesus in appearance: "He has no stately form or majesty that we should look upon Him, nor appearance that we should be attracted to Him." Jesus certainly understands when I've felt inferior, yet He knew exactly His position without being arrogant. Philippians 2:5–7 gives us His clear example of humility: "Have this attitude in yourselves which was also in Christ Jesus, who, although He existed in the form of God, did not regard equality with God a thing to be grasped, but emptied Himself, taking the form of a bond-servant, and being made in the likeness of men." At the right time, God exalted Jesus, and every knee will bow to His great name (vv. 9–11).

I know that many of you understand what it means to be rejected. Probably most of you. If you haven't yet, you will. It's inevitable. The key is in how we respond to rejection. Will we humble ourselves like Jesus? Or will we let pride and resentment get in the way so that we say, "Poor pitiful me," or, "It's not fair," or, "Nobody loves me"? Jesus loves you. God made you and knows you. He understands your pain. He accepts you and wants you to follow, trust, and obey Him. I wish I had learned this truth sooner than I did, but it is what it is. What matters now is that I allow the truth of God's Word and His character to set me free.

Wrong thinking really messes with God's intention that I live in truth. My mother once told me that no one would want to be around me if I wasn't "happy" all the time. I should smile, never show sadness or anger, and basically present the façade of having it all together. This wrong thinking led me to hide my true feelings from others. I was not transparent or real to anyone until a counselor helped me see that God accepts me just as I am. I don't have to pretend with Him.

It is crucial to mention throughout my story that my own thoughts and reactions for many years led to a self-destructive lifestyle of rejecting truth from God. Essentially, I lived a life independent of Him. When wrong thinking becomes rooted in our lives, what exactly does that mean? Consider roots from a botanist's perspective. Roots absorb water and nutrients for plants, anchor plants in the ground, and store extra food when needed. A gardener hopes to see desired plants take root instead of weeds because once a root goes deep, it's difficult to pull up.

I wish I had pulled out the roots of bitterness, anger, despair, and entitlement in the beginning before they were strong, when they weren't so deeply rooted. However, I chose to nurture and allow those roots to strengthen and deepen until it became more of a challenge to rip them out of my life. Reading, meditating on, and applying Scripture are necessary to change thought patterns and live in truth. Planting your roots in God's Word changes everything.

> How blessed is the man who does not walk in the counsel
> of the wicked, nor stand in the path of sinners, nor sit in the
> seat of scoffers! But his delight is in the law of the LORD, and
> in His law he meditates day and night. He will be like a tree
> firmly planted by streams of water, which yields its fruit in its

season and its leaf does not wither; and in whatever he does,
he prospers. —Psalm 1:1–3

I wish I could say that I relied on the Living Water to nourish me in my childhood and even into my forties, but thankfully, God did not give up on me! He reached out and drew me to Himself, the Living Water, and began to teach me to delight in Him and His Word. He taught me to seek Him.

The walls of my fortress continued to rise and imprison me as a young, single adult. So I tried to rescue myself with a survival technique of human nature—fierce independence. My quick answer to my plight became a successful career. But I had to find out the hard way that my career or education would not fill the emptiness that rejection had left behind.

CHAPTER 6

Longing for Escape

There are significant events and markers in our lives that often define us, whether we want them to or not. It could be a move, a tragedy, an unexpected good thing, a new job—anything that sets us in a direction that wasn't necessarily foreseen or planned. I like things to be neat and orderly, as many of us do, but life is messy and chaotic for the most part.

I was living at home in order to save money after graduating from college and while trying to fulfill the required clinical hours to attend the PA program at Duke. My father walked in the door after a doctor's appointment, and I could tell that he wasn't feeling well, as had been the case for a few months. He had a high fever and his blood pressure was extremely elevated. His doctor had strongly urged him to be hospitalized, but he refused.

I was concerned when he went to his bedroom, announcing that he was going to lie down for a little while. I followed my dad, insisting that I take his blood pressure and temperature. When I discovered that he truly wasn't well, I begged him to go to the hospital. He relented, so I called 911 and then my mother to alert her that an ambulance would be coming to get him. A terrible feeling came over me as I watched at the door for the rescue squad, wondering why it was taking so long. Mom arrived quickly from work and went straight to his bedroom. The next thing I knew, my mother screamed, so I raced back to their bedroom. He was not breathing, and there was no pulse. I pulled him from the bed onto the floor so that I could perform CPR. Because of my mother's panicked state, I insisted she leave the room. I needed her out so that I could think as I tried to save my dad's life. In between breaths, I pleaded with him, "Please don't leave me!"

The paramedics finally came. I continued to breathe for my father while a medic performed chest compressions. At that time, they did not carry a defibrillator to shock his heart. They loaded him into the ambulance and worked on him all the way to the hospital, but there was nothing that could be done to save his life. My brother was in Philadelphia, and calling him to report our father was dead was one of the hardest things I've ever done.

My father was only 55 years old when he died, and I was 23. The loss of my dad shut my mother down emotionally, and most of the details of planning his funeral fell on me. I called my dear friend and college room-mate to let her know what happened, and she immediately came to support me. Those days were a blur, but my father's death became a major marker in my life that affected my time, options, responsibilities, and outlook on life. In many ways, I felt like a victim of the circumstances around me. And I felt alone.

The years that followed were transitional with my mother in many ways, especially in my relationship with her. My brother and I took turns living with her during the last 10 years of her life. When he couldn't be there, I was there.

After finally getting my 2,000 hours of clinical experience, I was accepted at Duke in 1982 to get my PA degree, which I did over the next two years, often coming home on weekends. I got a job at Bowman Gray School of Medicine in Winston-Salem, North Carolina, in the medical school's hematology-oncology clinic upon graduation and continued to go home on weekends to be with my mom. I spent enough time in the car to listen to sermons from pastors like Charles Stanley. My understanding of God increased, and my faith began to grow. I was reminded over and over that God had the best plan, and if that meant I had to ask Him if I needed to leave Bowman Gray so I could be closer to my mother, I would.

I had never asked God for a sign before, but I asked Him to give me a rainbow when it was time to leave. I was young when I asked God this request and didn't have the spiritual maturity to know that seeking these sorts of signs is not something I'd recommend today (see Matthew 12:39; 16:4). More than a year had passed, and it was a time of drought in the area. No significant rain had fallen on North Carolina for weeks, so the possibility of seeing a rainbow was next to none. I was driving Interstate 40 on one of my many treks between where I lived during the week and my mother's house. It was oppressively hot. I glanced in my rearview mirror and, unexpectedly, there was the brightest, boldest rainbow I had ever seen. It was definitely acrylic, not watercolor. That was my rainbow—God's promise fulfilled to let me know that it was time for me to move on from my job.

Immediately, I began to look for a new job because that's what I thought I was supposed to do. I sincerely felt like God was leading me to put in my resignation as soon as possible. I felt peace about it, too. Psalm 32:8 spoke to me concerning His instruction in my life. He would teach me the way to go. And He was worthy of my trust. So I turned in my resignation. My supervisor asked me to give her six weeks so that she could find a replacement.

Three weeks went by with not a single indication of what my new job would be. I had no idea where I was going, but I prayed every day that God would make His way clear.

On the third weekend, a friend of mine, who was also a PA, called me about a job opportunity in South Carolina, a 20-minute drive from Charlotte, North Carolina. The job was in the emergency room, a place I desired to work. Without even knowing the salary, I went in for an interview and accepted the job on the spot. It actually doubled my salary and put me closer to my mother's house. There was no doubt: trusting God had brought me to a point of being confident this job was His will for my life. For the next few years, I was able to check on my mother more frequently, which gave me peace of mind. By 1993 and in my thirties, however, it was time for me to move back into my mom's home so that I could give her more care daily. At this point, I was working in Charlotte as a PA in cardiology.

Living with my mother again as an adult was necessary, but I can't say that it was easy. My social life was nonexistent. It became evident to me that singleness might be for a lifetime, mainly because I had no opportunity or time to meet a potential spouse. I was comfortable with my career, but there was still a desire that I would have a husband one day. We often quote Psalm 37:4 about delighting ourselves in God and Him giving us all our desires, but where was the man I desired? Did he exist? Wasn't I delighting in God, or was I delighting in my desires for this man instead of God? I wanted a husband, plain and simple. I thought a man would solve all my problems, make me happy, and fill my needs, but God certainly wasn't committed to the time line I created. Had God forgotten me? For my own well-being and contentment, I tried to surrender to God this desire to marry over and over. I repeatedly reminded myself that Jesus must fill all my needs. But I was trying to do this in my own strength—at that point, I still liked to be in control.

Caring for my mother took most of my free time and an immense emotional commitment. In the early 1990s she developed primary progressive aphasia (PPA), a rare form of dementia, which progressed and eventually mimicked Alzheimer's. She needed me more and more as the years continued, and eventually, I became the mother. Life seemed unfair in many ways, and to be perfectly candid, it was not easy to still be young and in the role of caretaker. God's Word became my refuge out of desperation.

In Proverbs 2:8, I was assured that God would guard the path of justice and watch over my way. As a guard for me, He would protect and shield me when I faced difficulties. Everything would pass through His loving hands first. And if I received justice from Him, I could give it. In fact, I was expected to give it. God used His Word to gently reveal my own ambition and pride, and it floored me. The Lord was my strength, my saving defense when I was mistreated or misunderstood by my own aging mother who didn't have her full faculties. She wasn't aware that the things said to me were hurtful. She could not control her deteriorating state. But deep down, I was angry at her for leaving me emotionally. To cope with this difficulty, I worked with a counselor to help me release my anger and resist the urge to believe the things my mother said.

After three years of being her sole caretaker, my brother and his family were able to move back to North Carolina and take my place. They moved into the house with her, and I was free to move to an apartment one block from her house. In 1999, I moved briefly to South Carolina to attend a special arrhythmia school. In 2000, 20 years after my father's death and when I was 42 years old, my mother passed away. I was taking the arrhythmia final exam that morning, but I called my brother to check on my mother since her condition had deteriorated. He knew I was taking my exam that morning, so he didn't tell me that my mother had passed away during the night. After my exam, I called my brother again, and this time he told me that she had died. Frankly, I was relieved since she had suffered a long time. I knew that I would miss her, but in many ways, she and I were both free. She was released from pain; I was released from watching her suffer.

Living in isolation can take on many forms. For me, my circumstances certainly gave cause for the alienation that I felt; however, getting comfortable in isolation became my own doing. I needed to heal, but I was fearful of the rejection that had plagued me since childhood. I grabbed on to verses like Psalm 30:2, "O LORD my God, I cried to You for help, and You healed me" and 68:20, "God is to us a God of deliverances; and to God the Lord belong escapes from death." I wanted to escape, but would I hold on to my chains because I was simply afraid to face the world, a life with God alone, and the possibility that my dreams may not come true? Had God forgotten me?

One thing I knew for sure—I wanted to get away from North Carolina and simply start over. I was exhausted with life. So, within two years, this southern girl eventually moved to the northern part of the Midwest with a company that would launch me to a crisis of belief.

CHAPTER 7

The Danger of Not Listening

What would it look like if we could get every detail of our lives right the first time? I've often wondered if it were even possible. I've come to the conclusion that we are bound to make mistakes. Perhaps the main advantage to making mistakes is that we have the chance to learn from them, and choosing to learn and change reveals more about our character than making the mistake.

Finding God's will is a topic that often consumes Christians. There are hundreds of books, Bible studies, and lectures on the topic. It seems like everyone has an opinion or agrees with an opinion as to how to accomplish this goal of the Christian life. I've read plenty of books on the topic, and I probably still have missed God's will at times in my life. Following God's will does not guarantee success. Failure can be His planned will for us in order to draw us closer to Him or to teach us something. To fail does not mean that I'm a failure. But what I've learned is that it's just as important to figure out God's will in some major event in my life as it is to obey God daily in the little things. Daily obedience has far more of an impact. If we obey daily, when major decisions arise, it's not such a big deal. I've learned this concept the hard way—more than once. *Why do I learn the hard way?* Because of my childhood and perhaps my nature, it is easier to be self-reliant. Being independent may help in basic survival skills, but as a Christian, it can be quite dangerous. I had a lot to learn about being totally dependent upon God and listening to Him.

Working for a new company and not having the shared responsibility for the care of my mother, I found myself evaluating my life. My new home was a place of snow, ice, and frigid temperatures more than 900 miles from my hometown. Let's just say one has a lot of time to think inside an apartment because it's too cold to venture outside unless absolutely necessary. Southern transplants do not do well in subzero weather, but I couldn't complain. A new location meant freedom from a life that I wanted to put out of my mind.

Up to this point, I'd spent much of my life focused on all the things I didn't have, such as companionship, love, security in my appearance, a social life, and purpose. It had not occurred to me how self-absorbed I was. Perhaps without a partner, I had no one to balance me, but that was no excuse. So I learned the hard way, for the most part, that God will find a way to make His children more like Him and totally dependent on Him.

My new job was nonclinical but enjoyable, regardless of the weather. No longer working as a PA, I was involved in launching a new implantable device. One of my responsibilities was to help the field sales force understand how the device worked and which particular patients would benefit from it. Intimidating at times to say the least, I learned to train others and found my niche.

One particularly difficult day, however, I was walking to my car in the parking lot of my company. It was snowing—basically, a day when no one in her right mind should be outside. I was homesick, although I had absolutely no home in North Carolina since my mother passed. Opening my car door, I sat down behind the wheel and thought, *What in the world am I doing? And what am I doing here?*

I picked up my cell phone and called the counseling center at First Baptist Atlanta. Maybe it was loneliness, grief, or panic, but I needed to talk to someone. A counselor answered the phone, and I spilled everything that was on my mind and in my heart. She listened and was very patient, but she finally asked me a haunting question, "If God took everything from you—your job, health, remaining family, and finances—in order to bring you close to Him, would it be worth it?" I knew the answer I should give was, "Yes," but I found myself being totally honest. I told her, "No." I walked back into the office building to my cubicle and sat there in a daze. I was totally ashamed at my response. I preferred temporary things rather than closeness with God. Pathetic, I know. But at least I was being honest and had a desire to say yes and mean it. Would God take everything from me? Already, I felt like so much was missing in my life, but would I be willing to surrender everything valuable to me—my career, my ambition, and even my desire for a husband? As a single woman close to hitting 45, I felt like I was in charge of my life rather than God. That wasn't God's fault, but mine alone.

My shame was on my mind, and I didn't get much work done that afternoon. Upon arrival at my apartment, I fell on my knees and cried to the Lord that it would be worth it to be closer to Him, even if I lost everything. So I pleaded, *Take it all, Lord.* Crawling into bed, exhaustion overcame me but so did a sense of peace. I trusted Him with my future.

Not long after my prayer, my boss offered me an opportunity of a lifetime. Europe always interested me, and since I had not been able to study in England all those years ago, my heart longed to work overseas. Ephesians 3:20 reminds us that He is "able to do far more abundantly beyond all that we ask or think." That's what He did for me. Four years earlier, I thought, *I might like to go to Europe one day,* and felt like God assured me in a time of prayer one morning that I would. My company's European headquarters happened to be in a country I wanted to visit. When my boss asked if I would like to move there for three years as an expatriate, I could hardly believe it. My dreams were coming true! I was slowly learning what it meant to trust God with everything, and if God wanted to send me to Europe, I was ready. Or at least I thought so. Would I really trust God?

When my plane landed at an airport in Europe, I might as well have landed on Mars. Everything was different, including the languages I heard blaring as announcements or being spoken by the people around me. Goodness, I was not in Kansas anymore! Fear and anxiety crept up, and I knew that there was no way I could make it unless God carried me on His shoulders.

My job was to lead an educational team for this new device. I was put in charge of training the sales and technical support teams. I also had to make sure that the doctors implanting the device knew how to successfully implant it. My area of responsibility covered Europe, the Middle East, and Africa. The reality of having to be totally dependent on Him became more evident. Was I really ready for it? He had brought me this far. Looking back over my life, I finally understood why my life took the turns it had.

Even with the cultural adjustments, what could compare to the beautiful scenery I saw every day from the window in my apartment? The Alps, in all their splendor, shouted of the majesty of God. I couldn't help but think of passages like Psalm 121:

> I will lift up my eyes to the mountains; from where shall my help come? My help comes from the LORD, who made heaven and earth. He will not allow your foot to slip; He who keeps you will not slumber. Behold, He who keeps Israel will neither slumber nor sleep. The LORD is your keeper; the LORD is your shade on your right hand. The sun will not smite you by day, nor the moon by night. The LORD will protect you from all evil; He will keep your soul. The LORD will guard your going out and your coming in from this time forth and forever.

My help to live in another country and a new culture would only come from God. He would have to help me face an extremely challenging job. He promised to keep me and guard me. My responsibility was to lift my eyes up to Him and keep my eyes on Him.

He became my refuge. Each morning, I sat in a chair by a big window that looked out upon those snow-covered mountains, read His Word, and talked to Him. It was my own private retreat. It was in that chair that I poured out my heart, my fears, my praise, and my dreams to Him. Jesus filled the loneliness with His companionship.

One of my concerns for the program when I arrived was that we didn't have a team of people to help me train. It became evident that I couldn't do the job alone. I took this request to the Lord, and within a month of being there, the company allowed me to hire more people to form my team. Within 22 months of my arrival, God had completely worked out the details for a successful program, and the company was improving their sales in Europe. He was always one step ahead of me working things out behind the scenes.

After two years of success and recognitions, even getting awards from the company, my pride crept up and things started to go downward. I became prideful without realizing it, and when I did, the peaceful life I had experienced evaporated. God cares about how we live and represent Him daily. Suddenly, I wasn't putting Him first or obeying Him in the little things. I continued to have time with God every morning, but I was simply reading, not engaging with His Word. I had become exactly what James 1:23–24 warned me not to be:

> For if anyone is a hearer of the word and not a doer, he is like a man who looks at his natural face in a mirror; for once he has looked at himself and gone away, he has immediately forgotten what kind of person he was.

My anxiety level began to increase due to the stressful demands of my job added to the fact that I missed my friends and family from home. I began to consider a return to the States. Had I made a mistake to come in the first place? My level of discontentment skyrocketed. The mistakes I chose to make snowballed because of my own pride. I wanted a higher salary and more recognition. I began to treat others less gently due to my frustrations with the stress. I found fault with Europe and sought a way to "get out of Dodge" as soon as possible, regardless of my contract to stay three years. There was a point, I admit, that in my spirit I knew what I was doing was wrong and disobedient to God, but I thought I was too far into the mess to repent and listen to the Lord. Big mistake.

My health started to deteriorate, and I developed metabolic syndrome, which symptoms include high blood pressure, prediabetes, and high cholesterol—all conditions that lead to heart disease, stroke, and diabetes. I was a wreck! It's amazing what taking control of my life away from God and disobeying Him did to my health! Confusion about my profession dominated my thoughts, and I really began to question if it had been God's will for me to come to Europe. Satan was having a field day with me, but I didn't realize it at the time. I knew that I was miserable and wanted the fastest way out after two years. So I ran.

I sought a job in the States. I approached the person who formalized my contract and asked to be let out of my three-year commitment a year early since my task had been successful and was essentially complete. I was released hesitantly, and I immediately felt like I had made a mistake. I arranged a meeting with a colleague to discuss a new job, which would be a promotion, but after that meeting, I felt more confused about accepting the job. In fact, I knew in my heart that for whatever reason, God was telling me it would be a mistake to return to the States, but I didn't know how to go backward. A sick feeling in my stomach that I was disobeying God overwhelmed me. I should have listened to God's Word from Jeremiah 17:5–10:

> Thus says the LORD, "Cursed is the man who trusts in mankind and makes flesh his strength, and whose heart turns away from the LORD. For he will be like a bush in the desert and will not see when prosperity comes, but will live in stony wastes in the wilderness, a land of salt without inhabitant. Blessed is the man who trusts in the LORD and whose trust is the LORD. For he will be like a tree planted by the water, that extends its roots by a stream and will not fear when the heat comes; but

its leaves will be green, and it will not be anxious in a year of drought nor cease to yield fruit. The heart is more deceitful than all else and is desperately sick; who can understand it? I, the LORD, search the heart, I test the mind, even to give to each man according to his ways, according to the results of his deeds."

I wish I could tell you that I didn't choose to trust in man instead of God, that I repented of taking things into my own hands, but I didn't. I left Europe at the end of 2004 and moved to take a job in Atlanta, Georgia, even though I knew it was not the right thing to do. How did I know moving at this time was wrong? I had no peace; I knew I had made an emotional decision to leave instead of honoring my contract. I just wanted *out*. If there were one thing I could redo in my life, this deliberate disobedience would be it. With complete awareness, I turned away from God's direction in my life, and He let me do it. I chose not to listen to Him and took the other job. I cannot tell you how much I came to regret that decision.

The next few months were the worst of my life. It made me sick to know I had made a mistake. My career and spiritual life plummeted. I found myself working in corporate America where integrity is often questionable, greed is normal, accusations abound, and reputations are damaged. Before long, I was affected by my environment and hated the person I had become. I really did not know myself anymore. For several years, I continued in this job on a very slippery slope.

One day I woke up, and my circumstances took a turn for the worse. Someone in the company took me completely by surprise and accused me of something based on untruths. Desperate and needing redemption, I turned to the same Christian counselor for help. The counselor gave me advice that I didn't want to hear: "Stop defending yourself." At first, I thought she was crazy. "Surrender to the Lord," she said. "He was spat upon, falsely accused, and lied about, yet He did not defend Himself." She told me that Jesus was showing me only a little bit about what He had experienced.

I knew she was right. I had gotten myself into such a disaster, and I had no one to blame but myself. I had turned away from God's perfect will for my life when I left Europe, and I was reaping what I had sown.

During this very hard time, I was reading about King Jehoshaphat and his desperate prayer to the Lord to save his people from their enemy (2 Chronicles 20). Jahaziel, the prophet, gave him a word from the Lord not to be afraid, because the battle belonged to God, not him. When Jehoshaphat heard that God would win the battle for them, he and the people fell down with their faces to the ground and worshiped Him.

I had been trying to win so many battles on my own that I just wanted to fall on my face, too, so I did—right there on the carpet. I felt God saying to me, "Claudia, repent of your self-sufficiency. Let me fight for you. Let me be in charge. Just worship and trust me." For a long time, I believed that God took things from me—my family, my finances, my job, my reputation, my health—but He showed me that He wanted to give His sacred love, His guidance, and the constant comfort of His Spirit. He was drawing me closer to Him. The lightbulb came on, and truth was revealed to my heart.

Praise the Lord that He is a forgiving God, full of grace and mercy when we repent. He does not condemn us, but He loves us and tells us to "go, and . . . sin no more" (John 8:11 ESV). Right then, I turned back to God and surrendered my circumstances, my job, and my future to Jesus. My hope rested in Jesus alone.

Fired from my job at age 49, I knew that I could easily lose my house in Atlanta if I did not pay the mortgage. I was given severance pay for six months. Money was tight, but God's Word spoke to me clearly each time the offering plate was passed in my church:

> "Bring the whole tithe into the storehouse, so that there may be food in My house, and test Me now in this," says the Lord of hosts, "if I will not open for you the windows of heaven and pour out for you a blessing until it overflows." —Malachi 3:10

I would be disobedient to Him if I did not give 10 percent of my severance pay, and I was finished with being disobedient. So I prayed, *Lord, I trust You to meet my needs, so I will give what is Yours to You.* I had gotten myself into this mess, but I had to rely on Him to get me out of the pit. My responsibility was obedience to His Word.

With nothing to do during the day, I felt like God was telling me to study His Word, pray for wisdom, seek Him first, and volunteer my time at my church. I learned about a clinical PA position that was going to open up at a place where I worked before in Charlotte, North Carolina, but that wouldn't happen for six to nine months. In the meantime, my relationship with the Lord deepened as I sought Him. I remembered what my counselor had asked me all those years ago—would I be willing to lose everything if I could be close to God? At this point in my life, I could honestly say, "Yes!" My beliefs about God were no longer simply head knowledge but were now heart knowledge. Little by little, Jesus revealed truth to me about Himself and His Word.

At the end of the six months, as my severance ran out, I had a crisis of belief: would I trust Jesus and believe Him, or would I focus on my circumstances? My track record for depending on myself had not been successful, so this time, I turned to Jesus and asked Him to do His will in my life. As my bank account dwindled to almost nothing, during the scariest time of my life, I fell in love with my Savior, Jesus. It was worth losing my reputation and job to be in a close, personal relationship with Him.

One of the ugly things God had to purify from my life during this time concerned forgiveness. In my opinion, I was a victim of injustice—an injustice that inflicted severe pain on me. My human nature wanted to fight back and get revenge, certainly not to forgive.

One morning, I was reading Luke 6:28, "Bless those who curse you, and pray for those who mistreat you." Everything in my mind wanted to cry, "But Lord, look what happened to *me*! My life is ruined! How can I possibly pray a blessing on those who came against me?" This passage of Scripture came to mind:

> Then Peter came and said to Him, "Lord, how often shall my
> brother sin against me and I forgive him? Up to seven times?"
> Jesus said to him, "I do not say to you, up to seven times, but
> up to seventy times seven." —Matthew 18:21–22

How could I forgive those in my past who caused me pain? God commanded me to forgive. In fact, He told me to confess my unwillingness to forgive to Him. To be unforgiving is serious, and I had to take responsibility for my sin. Making my own decisions had not worked out for me, but could I really choose to forgive? One thing I knew, I didn't want to go back to the miserable state I was in when trying to be in control of my life instead of letting God be my King. I would not make that mistake again.

God, help me forgive. I confess that I have unforgiveness in my heart and it is a sin, I prayed. In Matthew 18, right after the passage on forgiving others, Jesus tells Peter a parable to clearly emphasize His meaning. A king wanted to collect debts owed him by his slaves. One particular slave owed him 10,000 talents. There was no way this slave could pay a debt that large, so the king ordered him and his family to be sold so that payment could be made. The slave, however, fell on his knees and begged the king to have patience for the payment. The king felt compassion. Not only did he release him, but he forgave him the entire debt! The slave, instead of rejoicing in this forgiveness, went straight to someone who owed him a small amount of money and demanded payment. When payment couldn't be made, despite the man's earnest pleas, the slave threw the man into prison.

The king found out about this and summoned the slave. When reminded that he had been forgiven a sum impossible to repay and questioned as to why he didn't show the same compassion, the king didn't wait for his slave's response. Instead, he turned the slave over to the torturers until the full amount could be paid. Jesus then tells Peter, "My heavenly Father will also do the same to you, if each of you does not forgive his brother *from your heart*" (Matthew 18:35, author's emphasis).

Oh, my goodness! How many times had God forgiven me? *OK. I get it, Lord.* So right then, I chose to forgive those in my past who had wronged me and prayed that God would give me a soft heart. I chose to forgive multiple times a day until I knew that I really had forgiven them from my heart. Grasping the truth of God's Word is the key to moving past pain toward forgiveness. The truth of Romans 5:8 rooted deep in my heart: "But God demonstrates His own love toward us, in that while we were yet sinners, Christ died for us." Who was I to take revenge on another when I was a sinner, too? God not only died for me, but He died for all. I had so much to learn.

As I began to scrape the bottom of my bank account, I received a call that the PA job in North Carolina had opened up sooner than expected. Thankful for the job, this position created a new dilemma: my house in Atlanta didn't sell quickly. So I called some of my friends and arranged a schedule to sleep in various homes in Charlotte on the days that I worked as a clinical PA. I couldn't afford rent until my house sold. Despite the commute, returning to be a PA, seeing the kindness of old friends, and immersing myself on weekends in a church that taught God's Word and fostered vibrant community, I began to heal.

His lesson for me during this time was simple. He had not promised that I would be successful in life. Instead, He was going to conform me to the image of His Son, whatever means it took. I am the clay in His hands to do as He pleases. Obedience is more important than anything else to Him. My love and trust in Him are only shown through obedience to His Word and what I know He is telling me to do or not do. Disobedience severs our communication with God. I never wanted to miss His voice in my life again.

People have asked me, "How do you discern God's voice?" When you hear someone call your name, do you know who it is without seeing her or him? You do, if you know that person well. It is the same with Jesus. By spending time with Jesus and His Word, you can know Him. God says in Psalm 32:8, "I will instruct you and teach you in the way which you should go; I will counsel you with My eye upon you." God never goes against His Word. If I believe God is telling me to do something, it will never conflict with His Word or His nature. He gives me peace when I'm following Him, not confusion or doubt like I felt when I chose to leave Europe. Satan is the author of fear and confusion, and he wants to distract us from following God's will. I know that personally. I remind myself all the time that God will never leave me (Hebrews 13:5). God blesses obedience. Period. When and how is up to Him. It is not up to me to decide what the blessing will be or when I will receive it. I have learned to stand confidently in my relationship with Jesus. He will give me a strong sense of "stop" when I shouldn't do something, and He will reveal verses in His Word to also confirm His will.

For me, God used the pain and loss due to my poor decisions to expose what was in my heart. He began to strip me of my pride by allowing me to fall low. I had succeeded in the task I had been given in the company, but I failed at representing my Savior and Lord as I should have. He also used pain to bring me closer to Him. I heard a pastor once say, "You can tell if you are growing in grace and in your closeness to Jesus Christ if you look at how long it takes you to forgive an offense. Does it take years or months to forgive an offense when bitterness and anger set in or does it take days, hours, or better yet, minutes?"

During this time of testing and when I returned to take refuge in the strong arms of my Lord, God showed me Psalm 91:14–16. I wrote it out on a piece of paper and inserted my name into it and read it out loud to the Lord often as a declaration of my faith:

> Because [Claudia] has loved Me, therefore I will deliver [her]; I will set [Claudia] securely on high, because [she] has known My name. [Claudia] will call upon Me, and I will answer [her]; I will be with [Claudia] in trouble; I will rescue [her] and honor [her]. With a long life I will satisfy [Claudia] and let [her] see my salvation.

Did I deserve His deliverance? No. Did He love me, and does He love me now anyway? Absolutely.

God loves us. He forgives us. He doesn't condemn us. He tells us to repent of our sins and follow Him. That's it. I would follow Him. If it meant I would be penniless, single, without family, or without success, I came to the point in my life where it was Jesus or nothing. Jesus became my Prince. Jesus chose me when He died on the Cross. That's all that mattered.

My house in Atlanta would not sell. After seven months of driving to Charlotte to work three 12-hour shifts and then returning to Atlanta to wash clothes, go to church, and rest for three days, I realized that I couldn't continue to expect my kind friends to house me. So I started looking for a job in Atlanta. Although I didn't know the future, God certainly did—and it would change my life forever.

CHAPTER 8

Putting the Pieces Back Together

Emergency room personnel see a lot of open wounds. Sometimes these wounds are from the previous day, but most often they are from an injury that occurred in the past hour or so. There are a few steps one takes to treat a wound. The first thing: assess when it occurred, if the bleeding is controlled, where the wound is, what structures have been affected around the wound, and how deep it is. After assessment, the focus is on how to close the wound. Does it require layers of closure or simple closure? Generally, Lidocaine is used to numb the area before closing the wound. Once numb, the wound is cleaned with something that will kill any bacteria and remove all impurities so that no infection will occur. Then the wound is closed. Finally, pain medicine is given, if necessary. Typically, a wound will heal nicely with minimal evidence of a scar, if the scab is left alone.

If you are not medical or if you are squeamish, this description may have been too much information! I apologize, but those of us in the medical field deal with physical wounds every day, and we often forget that not everyone enjoys a gooey, gory story. Medical personnel talk about this kind of stuff over lunch—no problem!

The thing is, wounds from childhood, bad choices, abuse from others, and trials can be just as icky, infected, and serious. If a wound in our past is deep, it will bleed and hurt more. We want to stop the bleeding and pain immediately, so we try to put bandages on it and take pain medicine for a quick fix, which simply means we stuff down the issue for years rather than dealing with it immediately.

When physical wounds aren't treated properly, there is a high risk of infection. Typically, the infection in physical wounds spreads to the tissues closest to it. Likewise, infection in emotional wounds always spreads to the issues closest to it. When medical personnel are unable to close a physical wound in a given time frame, not only does the chance of infection increase, but often the body does the only thing it knows to do—try to heal the wound itself. Often this healing occurs from the inside out since it can't be properly cleaned and closed. When medical personnel finally tend the wound, other measures have to be taken, such as prescribing antibiotics and removing dead tissue so that it can be properly closed.

Interestingly, delaying the healing process is how many choose to heal and forgive an offense. When we delay our emotional healing from an offense by refusing to forgive, the chances of bitterness and anger increase, and unforgiveness deepens. Healing not only takes more time in this instance, but the scar is worse. Bitterness and anger affect other issues and other people in our lives, and this "infection" is seen easily in the person who refuses to forgive.

The scar of unforgiveness can be loss of relationships, health, or dreams. When we let offenses sit, and we do not forgive, repent, or obey, infection is bound to spread. When we offer grace and forgiveness to others, bitterness won't have the chance to take root. Bitterness is a deadly infection that spreads. It seeps in quickly, and its roots deepen the longer we try to ignore it. We tell ourselves nothing is wrong; we convince ourselves and others that we have forgiven, but our actions share another story. In addition, when we don't forgive ourselves or accept God's forgiveness, we risk falling into despair and turning from God. In essence, we are saying that Christ's death on the Cross was not enough to pay for our sins.

Sometimes a physical infection gets so severe that pus accumulates and the area has to be drained. Antibiotics aren't enough. Bitterness, anger, resentment, and a lack of forgiveness can take such deep root that a counselor may be needed to help dig out the roots of these problems. The quicker we disinfect and close a bleeding wound, the smaller the scar will be. God is the Great Physician who can heal our wounds and prevent large, ugly scars.

I had to learn the hard way that God could be strong for me in the areas in which I was the weakest. Today, the scars I have from my childhood and from mistakes I made in adulthood serve to remind me of that which I could not do on my own. I needed (and continue to need) God daily. My wounds have healed and are healing, but the scars remain. Perhaps scars fade with time, but seeing the scars reminds me what happens when I scramble to try to control and get what I want on my own and encourages me to regard God's voice and trust Him instead.

Though Jesus was sinless, He had the scars of the Cross. Even after He rose from the grave, He appeared to the disciples and held out His scarred hands for Thomas to see. Goodness, He could have erased those wounds since He healed the blind and the lame! But He chose to keep the scars on His hands as a testimony to us that He paid the price for us. "He was pierced because of our rebellions and crushed because of our crimes. He bore the punishment that made us whole; by his wounds we are healed" (Isaiah 53:5 CEB). He heals me from my sin because He died to pay the penalty of my rebellion.

My scars are still evident, but I do not look at them with shame anymore. I have been forgiven, and now I accept God's Word as truth and reject Satan's lies. Now, my scars motivate me to stay close to Him and to be thankful, as stated in 1 Thessalonians 5:18, "in everything give thanks; for this is God's will for you in Christ Jesus." My scars do not have to rob me of joy found in God alone. Once we allow the wounds to heal and become scars—a visible reminder but no longer raw—then we can say with confidence to those scars, "You are a reminder that I am not to elevate myself above God, but you are also proof that God has healed me." The scars do not have to define me anymore because I'm healed, and the truth has set me free.

There is something about age that gives enough experience to make us wiser, if we learn from our mistakes. Since you're still reading my story, you know I've made some big mistakes. I am desperate for God because without the filling of His Holy Spirit, I cannot possibly live the victorious, joyful, and abundant life that Christ intends for every believer.

God gives us opportunities to obey Him. He wants us to examine our hearts and see what is the most important thing in our lives because that will be where our heart is (Matthew 6:21). Tests and trials build endurance, if we respond according to His Word.

> Count it all joy, my brothers, when you meet trials of various kinds, for you know that the testing of your faith produces steadfastness. And let steadfastness have its full effect, that you may be perfect and complete, lacking in nothing.
> —James 1:2–4 ESV

Anytime we dwell on the past, it keeps us from moving forward. Isaiah 43:18 reminds us: "Remember not the former things, nor consider the things of old" (ESV). If I dwell on what I didn't do right, I'm still trapped in the past. The fact is that God has forgiven me. I laid my past at His feet and accepted His forgiveness. Now He wants me to face trials with joy and complete assurance that He is with me and will be my strength.

In *The Bible Exposition Commentary*, Warren Wiersbe says:

> If we value comfort more than character, then trials will upset us. If we value material and physical more than the spiritual, we will not be able to "count it all joy." If we live only for the present and forget the future, then trials will make us bitter, not better.

Job, who lost everything, had the right heart when he declared, "But He knows the way I take; when He has tried me, I shall come forth as gold" (Job 23:10).

Job endured through his trials. He knew that God would be faithful. It wasn't easy, but He ignored his wife's advice to "Curse God and die!" (Job 2:9). He chose to surrender himself to God no matter what.

I have no doubt that God forgave me for not listening to His voice in my past. I know the power of my God. My biggest challenge after I messed up was forgiving myself and not living under my own condemnation. It is easy to live a defeated Christian life, but it is not God's plan for any child of God to do so. "The thief comes only to steal and kill and destroy; I came that they may have life, and have it abundantly" (John 10:10). Satan's goal is to defeat Christians, but Jesus gives abundant life. Ephesians 3:20–21 reiterates this concept:

> Now to Him who is able to do far more abundantly beyond all that we ask or think, according to the power that works within us, to Him be the glory in the church and in Christ Jesus to all generations forever and ever.

I had to come to the end of myself by surrendering to Him and repenting. I had to take God at His Word, stop wallowing in guilt, and focus on Jesus. I had to accept grace and give it to others.

When I chose to surrender my brokenness to God, Psalm 40:1–3 became a reality in my life:

> He inclined to me and heard my cry. He brought me up out of the pit of destruction, out of the miry clay, and He set my feet upon a rock making my footsteps firm. He put a new song in my mouth, a song of praise to our God.

It was as if I was starting over with a clean slate. I cried out to God when I still found myself alone while most of my friends were married and had grown children. Psalm 62:5–6 became my present and future: "My soul, wait in silence for God only, for my hope is from Him. He only is my rock and my salvation, my stronghold; I shall not be shaken." As I've said, I learned the hard way, and with God's help, history will not ever repeat itself.

When we go through brokenness, God uses it to pull us to Him. Jeremiah 29:11–14 is clear about seeking God:

> "For I know the plans that I have for you," declares the LORD, "plans for welfare and not for calamity to give you a future and a hope. Then you will call upon Me and come and pray to Me, and I will listen to you. You will seek Me and find Me when you search for Me with all your heart. I will be found by you," declares the LORD, "and I will restore your fortunes and will gather you from all the nations and from all the places where I have driven you," declares the LORD, "and I will bring you back to the place from where I sent you into exile."

My brokenness brought me to a time of conviction, repentance, cleansing, seeking God with a whole heart, and obeying His Word. The biggest hindrance to blessing is disobedience. I knew that firsthand. I had to allow God to give me a soft heart, I had to forgive as God forgave me, and I determined to accept His will for me joyfully.

Being joyful is a choice every day. Our choice. Why do we put the blame on God and think He is holding out on us? Why do we think God doesn't want us to be happy? These are the same lies that Satan told Eve. We can never earn God's blessings. We always receive them undeservedly. But, He knows when we need them and when we can receive them as gifts instead of as idols.

Put these verses in the bank:

> "My grace is sufficient for you, for power is perfected in weakness." Most gladly, therefore, I will rather boast about my weaknesses, so that the power of Christ may dwell in

me. Therefore I am well content with weaknesses, with
insults, with distresses, with persecutions, with difficulties,
for Christ's sake; for when I am weak, then I am strong.
—2 Corinthians 12:9–10

His grace is enough. He is strong. I am weak. But I'll be honest. In my weakness, I still wasted too much energy on wanting a husband and trying to be successful in everything.

By the time I was 50, I was back in Atlanta working as a PA. My house had unexpectedly sold after I left my job in Charlotte, North Carolina, so I was no longer a homeowner but a renter in a basement apartment. And I still had no idea if God would fulfill my lifelong desire to be married. One thing I did know was the thought that a man could fulfill all my needs for companionship, happiness, and security was not going to consume my mind anymore. Jesus became the One who fulfilled me. If He chose to bring a man into my life, fine. Actually, that would be *more than fine*. But if not, that was fine, too. I was focusing on Him, and it felt good. Finally, it was enough to follow Jesus. With a determined heart, I looked to Proverbs 3:5–6 once again in my life: "Trust in the LORD with all your heart and do not lean on your own understanding. In all your ways acknowledge Him, and He will make your paths straight." So what if the path God showed me didn't make sense!

When God told Moses to cross the Red Sea, Moses had to take the first step and raise the staff to part the water. It seems like God told many people of the Bible to do something that made no sense. Noah, Esther, Gideon, Jesus' mother, Paul, and Peter are only a handful of examples. There are countless more in the Bible. If He did it then, what makes us think He won't ask His followers now to do something completely out of our comfort zone?

As I neared the age of 51, the surgeon I worked for asked me if I would consider going on a medical missions trip to Honduras. My first reaction was a resounding "No." I wanted to go but was scared to death! It was February, and he said the trip was in June. That was not enough time to get my act together to travel to a developing country. "This is not the time for me," I told him emphatically. He countered with, "Claudia, I personally will pay for your trip. And I won't even charge the time off as vacation time." He had originally planned to go but had to cancel. "At least call the doctor leading the trip to find out about it," he encouraged. Reluctantly, with no more excuses, I took the name of the contact.

Lord, why would you send me to Honduras when I hate intense heat, humidity, and bugs? I silently asked the Lord. Feeling coerced, I met with the missions trip physician who was coleading. He answered my questions and assured me that we would stay at an air-conditioned hotel. When I found out I wouldn't be staying in a tent, my barriers began to break down. I prayed about it, and my resolve not to go weakened. I knew without a doubt God was directing me to go. Being single gave me the freedom to travel and do adventurous things, but sometimes it also made me afraid. The team was not from my church, so these were new people to me. The doors to go kept opening, and finally I told the Lord I would go.

Would this be a defining moment in my life? Without knowing it, I was about to get a glimpse of what it meant to have an outward focus like Jesus instead of an inward focus like I was used to having.

CHAPTER 9

Following Jesus to Places Unknown

Arriving at the sending church of the Honduras missions trip, I saw my team members. I met some of them when we packed suitcases with medicine earlier, but didn't know them well. Excited, but also scared, I looked around to observe my team members. They didn't look nervous at all! And they were very friendly.

One registered nurse (RN) was very petite, extremely pleasant, and had a beautiful smile. Even though she was in her late fifties, she and her curly hair bounced around as she talked to everyone. Another woman, who was a pharmacy assistant, was a go-getter like me. I felt we would become good friends. There was a dentist who was the jokester of the group. Another dentist, who was not new to volunteering in missions, had the reputation of being able to fix his equipment with duct tape if necessary! Both of these dentists were patient, gentle, and dedicated to the call of God to use their skills overseas. The pharmacist on the team was quiet and worked hard to translate medication instructions into Spanish. A recovery room RN in her mid-sixties had pretty white hair and was calm, extremely kind, and levelheaded. A couple, who were former full-time missionaries in Mexico, were our primary interpreters on the trip. They smiled continually. The church missions pastor accompanied us, too. He was jovial, round-faced, stocky, and full of action. I could tell from the beginning that the oldest couple on the team, in their seventies, would be the "grandparents" of the group. They participated in many missions opportunities and knew their way around. They were kind and loving, and I looked forward to their company. Also included were a soft-spoken RN and an eccentric, retired RN, both who would prove valuable to the team as well. One more doctor was going, the other coleader, and he was known to have a heart for missions. I had not met him in the earlier meetings. It was quite a group of people with different personalities, skills, ages, and experience. I would be the learner; I was the newbie.

We had each packed one suitcase for personal use and would also carry one suitcase of medicine and supplies. My expectation was to help patients, but other than that, I didn't know what to expect. We got on a bus at the church in metro-Atlanta that would take us to the airport. Was I ready for this trip? How would I do? Would I be accepted by my team and be useful?

The moment I landed in Honduras, the sweat started to trickle. The airport was small and lacking in many modern amenities. I thought, *Oh, my goodness! What have I gotten myself into?* The local church pastors and the local missionary met us to take us to our hotel.

It took only one day to stop wearing makeup and styling my hair. Our team climbed into a well-used, air-conditioned bus to travel to the clinic site, going over the worst roads I had ever experienced. When we finally arrived, it was hard to take in what we saw. We were to conduct the clinic in cement stalls behind the church. There was no electricity in these stalls, and no air was moving. Nevertheless, scores of people lined up to be treated for eye, dental, or health issues on the first day of the clinic. The news of our arrival was out. It broke my heart to see so many extremely poor people who needed basic treatment, a kind word, and especially a Savior. Before the medical team saw a patient, he or she heard a gospel message from someone designated for that job.

One woman came to us with a large cut on her arm. She said that she had fallen on a piece of metal and needed stitches. Unfortunately, we did not have regular sutures with us, so I had to use dental sutures, which are extremely tiny. There were no sterile cloths to put around the wound, so we had to improvise. Standing outside in the heat, I placed her arm on a cement window opening of the stall. She was inside on the other side of the window in the shade. I initially poured Betadine solution on her arm and began to close the wound, praying the whole time. I had to use my fingers to hold the skin together, and mercifully one of my teammates put cold cloths on the back of my neck as I closed the laceration. Every time I made a stitch, one of the RNs poured Betadine on the wound. Because the environment wasn't sterile, I did not close the wound completely but left space for it to drain to hopefully prevent infection. The patient's husband watched, and one of our interpreters shared the story of Jesus with both of them as I sewed slowly. I wanted there to be enough time for the interpreter to share the gospel. When I finished, she and her husband gave their lives to Christ. I gave her an antibiotic with verbal instructions through the interpreter on how often to take the medicine.

The next day, I checked on her and found out how she really sustained her injury. Her husband had gotten mad and swung a machete at her! She lifted her arm to stop a fatal blow, causing the injury. Her husband felt such remorse that he brought her to the medical site and was open to hearing God's Word. God works miracles in mysterious ways. Hearing her story made an impact on my life, and I couldn't help but think what a blessing these people were to me. When you serve others, you don't think about yourself.

One day during the week, we were notified that a public transportation strike in the city and surrounding areas could cause a security problem for us. The highways were shut down, and we were warned that protesters were shooting at cars and buses on the roads. The medical site was only four miles from our hotel, and the morning we heard this news, we did a lot of praying on the bus! The driver took us on very bad back roads, and with God's protection, we arrived safely.

The quick bond with my team members was extraordinary. The meetings prior to the trip allowed me to meet many on the team, but now I was getting to know them as friends. Since I didn't have to participate in the skills performance meeting, however, I hadn't met both of the team doctors who led the missions trip. The doctor I had not met, Dr. David Cantrell, came to me during our first clinic day in Honduras with a patient who had a severe wound on his backside. The man had suffered a spinal cord injury and was confined to a wheelchair. A wound had formed from constantly sitting without proper care. An area the size of a softball had simply rotted, leaving a gaping and infected hole. I had never seen anything like it! The smell was overpowering, and the wound drained significantly. We examined him and knew the infection was serious. Red Cross was contacted to provide the patient transportation to the hospital. No ambulance was safe driving on the roads during the transportation strike. Dr. Cantrell took the patient inside the church and laid him on his side.

After a long day of seeing patients, I wanted to find out about the patient with the serious infection. I was informed that Red Cross had collected the man and that Dr. Cantrell had insisted on cleaning the man's wound himself, as well as the floor on which it had drained. Cleaning wounds, as well as drainage, is usually the job given to a nurse, but he would not let anyone else help him. Dr. Cantrell was certainly different than most physicians.

I have to say that I took notice of this gentle and humble man during the week. He was kind, soft-spoken, and had a caring, servant's heart. He was also kind of cute, mostly bald with big, beautiful blue eyes—even a twinkle in his eye when he laughed. We only spoke once during the entire seven-day trip, when he approached me about the man's wound, but I found myself noticing him often and was drawn to the way he treated people. When I asked about him, I was told that he was a widower and had two grown daughters.

Each night after treating patients, the Honduran church partner hosted an evangelistic service. Our team worshiped with Hondurans, and many of those who had been treated found hope in Christ. It was one of the most meaningful and joyous weeks of my life. We saw more than 1,800 patients, and a few hundred indicated that they decided to follow Jesus. Missions was no longer something that other Christians did—it was something I did—and wanted to do again, too!

When I returned home, I was exhausted but energized with new purpose. God took me way out of my comfort zone and sustained me. The heat was insignificant compared to the reward of serving others and seeing many decide to follow Jesus. But I also returned home thinking about Dr. Cantrell. My entire life I'd dreamed of marrying a godly, kind man. Here was one who was a few years older, unmarried, loved medical missions, and was humble, brilliant, and godly. I couldn't help it—I had the worst teenage crush on him that you could imagine. But one thing was for sure. If I were to even see him again, God would have to orchestrate it. I would not pursue Dr. David Cantrell.

A month after returning from Honduras, a few on the team met at a restaurant to debrief the trip and visit together. I didn't know if Dr. Cantrell would be there, yet he was, along with his daughter, Kelly, and her husband. Dr. Cantrell briefly introduced me to them, and I ended up sitting beside him during the meal. I was even able to talk to Kelly some. She was delightful. That night, my desire to know Dr. Cantrell was overwhelming, but I was not going down the road of getting my hopes up for a friendship.

My friends told me I needed to join a dating website, but I said no. For me, I didn't feel like that was God's plan. It wasn't like men weren't interested in me. One man took me out a few times, but it became obvious after a time of dating that he only wanted one thing—something I was unwilling to give. Long ago, I made a pledge that I would stay sexually pure and would not have sex outside of marriage. I was still a virgin and planned to stay that way as long as I was single. So if God wanted to bring a man into my life who would respect and love me and want to marry me, I was going to make sure I saved myself for him. God would have to change my marital status after all these years. I wasn't a spring chicken anymore—I had hit menopause age! So it was going to be God's timing or no timing.

I would not try to manipulate a way to see Dr. Cantrell. I did, however, pray that God would allow me to get to know him better and possibly date him if it was His will.

A year later in 2009, Dr. Cantrell and I ended up helping at LOVELOUD, a free community medical clinic hosted by First Baptist Church of Woodstock, Georgia. Although I saw him there, we never spoke. He seemed preoccupied. When I got in my car later that day to go home, I thought, *Claudia, he's never going to look at you.* So, I carried on with my life, my job, and my fresh perspective on serving for God's kingdom purposes. God had me in His hands.

I thought perhaps God wanted me to pursue medical missions, even thinking that I might become a medical missionary. An opportunity to serve with Mercy Ships for two weeks became a possibility, and I felt God's leading to pursue it. I was excited to follow this leading!

Leaving my job for even a short time wouldn't be easy, and it was frightening to think of going overseas again. But I called the Mercy Ships headquarters in Texas to speak to a recruiter. Upon speaking with her, I was informed that rather than going only two weeks, I had to stay three months. In addition, she told me that they were now requiring a medical doctor to be a first assist in surgery rather than a PA. I was so disappointed. I thanked her for the information and hung up the phone. I was confused. I felt like God led me to go after this opportunity.

On the same day, my phone rang. The recruiter told me that she had mentioned our conversation to another recruiter and was immediately informed that there was a two-week slot available in surgery that they had not been able to fill with a physician. However, this opportunity required orthopedic surgery experience. I had only informed her of my experience as a first assist in surgery, but had not told her my specialty of orthopedics! I had goose bumps and knew instantly this was what I was supposed to do. I prepared to go, arranged my flight, and spoke directly to the chief surgeon.

Quite unexpectedly, one month prior to leaving, I discovered I had a large ovarian cyst that had to be removed soon. After my surgeon told me that *soon* meant within the next few weeks, I began to cry. *Why, Lord, did you tell me to pursue Mercy Ships and then take it away from me?* His answer was again very clear—*trust Me.*

God knew the big picture during my disappointment. Minding my own business, and not long after the Mercy Ships opportunity fell through, I had another chance encounter with Dr. David Cantrell.

CHAPTER 10

Sweet Dreams

I love having a good dream. Everything is happy and resolving well, it's warm and snuggly under the covers, and all of a sudden, you feel yourself waking up. You do your best not to be pulled away from the sweet dream, but even closing your eyes tight so that the morning light is pushed back, you can't keep the day from dawning. *Just a few more minutes.* But alas, the dream fades and you wonder, *Was that real or was my subconscious playing out a fantastic but cruel joke on me?*

This is exactly how I felt after walking out of a grocery store, more than 18 months after the missions trip to Honduras. I was standing at the pharmacy counter of my regular grocery store finishing up a transaction. When I turned around to leave the store, I nearly ran smack into Dr. Cantrell—David. Apparently he had seen me and waited patiently until I finished. We talked for a minute and then I said, "Call me sometime, and we'll catch up." On cloud nine, I left the store feeling like maybe he would call. I was hoping he would.

But he didn't. For the next few months, I prayed, *God, if David is supposed to be in my life, let me meet up with him again.* Occasionally, I would stop by the grocery store, but I didn't run into him. I knew that he probably had a lot of things on his plate, especially because I had heard that his daughter, Kelly, had cancer.

One afternoon in June 2010, several months since I last saw David, I stopped at my regular grocery store. As I was coming out, I heard someone call my name. It was David. I hardly recognized him because he had on a ball cap. Oh my goodness! I found myself thinking, *What in the world do I look like?* We chatted for about ten minutes. Of course, I was so nervous that I did most of the talking. When it was time to go to our cars, we parted. He didn't ask for my phone number, I didn't fall at his feet, and I got in the car and felt like beating my head on the steering wheel. All I could think was . . . *I. Am. So. Stupid.*

In January 2011, about seven months after the second chance run-in with David at the grocery store, a friend told me that Kelly had died. My heart hurt for David. To offer condolences, I called him to give my sympathy for his loss and to offer to bring by some brownies. His grief was obvious. He asked me to bring the brownies by his office and leave them with his staff. And then he politely thanked me and ended the conversation.

Since the missions trip, I had been praying for this man, but I realized that day that I had to let go of any idea of getting to know him better. I was done. He wasn't interested in me, even as a friend. A while after this encounter, I heard that he was dating someone. I got in my car after work, started crying, and told God, *I need to leave this city. I can't be in Atlanta anymore. I can't be in a place where I will think about David or possibly run into him.* I totally released the dream of David. In that moment, I decided that if God would give me a peace about moving back to Charlotte, I would. So I continued to pray about leaving over the next couple of months. God gave me the peace I needed.

A PA job in Charlotte came to my attention, and I accepted. I gave a ten-week notice for my job in Atlanta and drove up to Charlotte to look for a house. David apparently was no longer an option. That door was slammed shut. There was no doubt God was moving me to Charlotte, and it was a relief. I was 53. It was time to face the fact that I would most likely be single the rest of my life. My life was surrendered to the Lord; the dream of David was let go.

Six weeks before I was to move to Charlotte, a month into my resignation, I found a sticky note on my computer at work saying that Dr. David Cantrell had called. Mouth-open shock does not adequately express my surprise.

It's time for you to get part of the story from this wonderful man himself.

God is the God of surprises at times, and I've had my share of unexpected twists and turns. My first wife died after we had been married for 33 years. She had multiple sclerosis for ten years, starting in 1995, and progressively she became disabled. Our two daughters, Kelly and Katie, helped with her care, as did our young niece, who lived with us at the time. Between practicing medicine, caring for my wife, and driving my niece to after-school activities, my life was definitely ordered with not a minute to spare. One afternoon, Katie was home with friends, and my wife had a stroke. Although everything was done for her, she never recovered and died after three weeks. When she died, I found myself single and in my early fifties. I had no desire to ever get married again. I was exhausted.

Without the restraints of caring for someone, I became interested in medical missions trip opportunities through my church, First Baptist of Woodstock. My life outside of the office was at the church with choir and a men's Sunday School class. So, of course, I heard about missions opportunities. I first went to Honduras in 2007 and then helped coordinate another medical missions trip to Honduras the next year. It was on the second trip to Honduras that I noticed a PA named Claudia. I was impressed with her knowledge and passion for medicine. I thought she was pretty, but I wasn't interested in pursuing any kind of relationship. I occasionally dated, at the insistence of a friend, but marriage was not in my long-range goals. I'm an out-of-sight, out-of-mind kind of guy, so after the missions trip, I had other things on my mind besides Claudia.

A missions trip to Ukraine came to my attention in 2009. When I returned from that trip, my world fell apart: a diagnosis of cancer for Kelly, my daughter. I ran into Claudia again at our church's LOVELOUD event where medical expertise is donated freely to indigent patients. I could not talk to her, however, because my life was centered around Kelly at that time. I ran into Claudia in the grocery store on two occasions. My interest was piqued, but I didn't have time to deviate from my focus on Kelly. Kelly met Claudia shortly after the missions trip to Honduras where I had initially met Claudia. Several times afterward, Kelly asked me about Claudia and encouraged me to contact her. She was worried about her husband and me and kept telling us that we both needed to remarry if she died. She was adamant that we find happiness again. I think she saw the toll her illness took on both of us. At that time, I couldn't think of anything but Kelly.

After Kelly died in January of 2011, I was in a daze. People brought food, sent flowers and cards, and checked on me. Even Claudia brought brownies by the office. But I was numb. I worked. Several months later when I came out of the haze, I started thinking about Claudia. I had given myself five months to grieve Kelly, but I remembered that Kelly kept mentioning Claudia before she died. Even one of my patients knew Claudia and told me that I should take her out on a date. I actually couldn't get her off my mind. Finally, I went out on a limb and tried to find her phone number. I looked up her work website and found the office number. Before I lost my nerve, I called during my lunch hour. She was out to lunch, so I had to leave a message with the receptionist. When she returned my call later that day, I think she thought I was calling about another missions trip opportunity because she said, "What can I do for you?" We had not seen each other in a year. My skill at asking a woman out on a date was lacking, and I wasn't sure she would even accept. I asked her if she would like to go to dinner with me. Boy, was she ever surprised! I couldn't believe she agreed.

Several incoherent thoughts invaded my head immediately when I saw that sticky note. *Call Dr. David Cantrell.* I took a few deep breaths. I decided he was most likely calling me about another missions trip. *Surely that was it.* I pulled myself together and dialed his number.

We talked for a couple of minutes, and it was a little awkward. I wasn't sure why he called. So I asked, "What can I do for you?" And that's when he asked if I'd like to go to dinner. You could have knocked me over with a feather! I responded, "Absolutely." We set a date for the coming weekend, and then I hung up the phone, stunned but elated. David Cantrell asked me on a date—a date I had waited three years for!

But I'm moving to North Carolina! I have a contract on a house in Charlotte! God, Your timing is really off this time! I couldn't believe it. Here was the specific man I had dreamed about for three years, and finally he was asking me out when I was about to move. Actually I had been dreaming about this type of man for 30 years! Could life get any more unbelievable? Was God's timing off? How would I tell him I was about to move? But there was no doubt, even though David unexpectedly contacted me, God's will for me was to move back to Charlotte. I knew I had to trust God and be loyal to Him rather than my desires. I kept Hosea 6:6 close to my heart, "For I delight in loyalty rather than sacrifice." Surely, God had something more to teach me. If that included David or not, so be it. But I had a date scheduled with Dr. Cantrell.

CHAPTER 11

God's Plan and Grocery Stores

The night came for me to take Claudia out. I was excited. It was July 1, 2011. I decided we would go by Marietta Square's "Art in the Park" first. It didn't occur to me how hot it would be when I made the plans. I picked her up, and we walked around the event for a while. I kept thinking about the heat and was worried that she was thinking the same thing. We ducked in and out of antique shops just to be in air-conditioning.

We decided to ditch the browsing and go to supper. I took her to Stoney River Steakhouse and Grill at a local mall. We had not even been sitting at the table for five minutes when Claudia mentioned that she was moving to Charlotte. She had already bought a house. Of all the luck! Why did I wait so long to ask her out? I couldn't believe it. So I smiled and nodded my head despite feeling disappointed.

After dinner, I took her back home, and we sat outside and talked until

1:30 a.m. I listened to her new plans. She would be moving in six weeks.

I got in the car to drive home and thought, *God, what am I doing here?* So for four weeks, I didn't call her, and she didn't call me. What was the point? But, no matter how hard I tried, I couldn't stop thinking about her.

When David didn't call me after our date, I was very disappointed, but like I said, I was not going to pursue him. I was moving to Charlotte, so that was that. I had my marching orders from God, and I was not going to disobey Him. I had enough experience in the past with disobedience, and I didn't want to go there. End of story. David knew my number if he wanted to call.

Two weeks before I moved, I participated in a joint replacement surgery, as was a normal part of my job, and had to wear a hazmat suit and helmet. Even though the helmet smashed my hair to my head and most of my makeup rubbed off, I needed to stop by the grocery store after work. I really didn't want to run into David, so I intentionally drove five miles out of my way to another grocery store. As I was checking out, I looked up and jumped. David was standing at the edge of my shopping cart! What was it with me, David, and grocery stores?!

He said, "What are you doing at this store?"

I said the first thing that came to my mind. "It's the best store to buy diet bars." *I could not believe I said that.* Then I said, "I'm moving in two weeks."

"I know," he replied.

"Why don't you let me cook for you before I leave?" I said on the spur of the moment.

He agreed, but he also mentioned that he would like to take me for a drive to Chattanooga, Tennessee, in his convertible.

I didn't expect to see Claudia in the grocery store, but perhaps, secretly, I was hoping I would, even though it wasn't our normal grocery store. Her hair looked a little funny, but to me, she was beautiful. She acted pleased to see me. We started talking, and she mentioned that she was moving in two weeks. There's no doubt that we both felt some sort of attraction to each other, and when she offered to cook a meal for me before she moved, I suggested that we take a drive to Chattanooga, too.

A few days later, I went to her home for a meal. I was nervous because I really wanted to ask her to meet my youngest daughter, Katie. I mentioned that Katie might want to be a PA one day, not knowing if she was really interested in that or not, but I felt like I needed an excuse to invite Claudia to meet my daughter.

Later that week, Claudia came over. I introduced her to Katie and our dog, Beau. Claudia was liked by both. Not only did Katie and Claudia hit it off well, but I think Beau liked her better than me!

A couple days later, I picked Claudia up for our day in Chattanooga. The drive is about an hour and a half from Marietta, but I wanted her to see the city where my first wife and I raised our daughters and where I did my residency. We went to a craft fair, saw some sights, and stayed to listen to a band playing by the river. We set up chairs, and even though it started to rain, we listened to music for an hour. We felt comfortable around each other, and I felt contentment like I hadn't felt before.

It was a late drive back to Marietta; the clock passed midnight and Claudia told me that it was her birthday—August 14. I had no idea. I wanted to buy her something at the craft show, but she wouldn't let me. Of course, then I wished I had.

I didn't want her to move. We were just starting to get to know each other. I offered to help her pack, but she said that she could do it herself. How on earth was I going to see her again? I fell in love with her in Chattanooga.

Walking out of church on my birthday, after the wonderful Chattanooga date with David, I couldn't believe I refused his offer to help me pack. Simply put, I was scared to death. I was attracted to him, but the reality remained that I was moving four hours away. It was easy to see the walls of self-preservation going up fast around my heart. I didn't feel like a relationship could go anywhere if I lived in Charlotte. I asked God if I was being too cautious, if I should have allowed David to help me pack. I missed him already! Before I knew what I was doing, I called him and said, "Please come help me pack."

I couldn't believe Claudia called me and welcomed my help packing. After that phone call, I made a plan. I sat down and wrote a few romantic notes to secretly plant in her moving boxes. Even though I was way out of practice in wooing a woman, I knew this was something I could do to get her attention and make her feel special. I wanted her to know this was more than a passing interest for me, and there was no doubt in my mind that God put her on my heart.

So without her knowing, I snuck the cards in some boxes. I couldn't wait for Claudia to get to Charlotte to find them!

David came over to help me pack, and he was awfully chipper. Was he happy I was moving? I had no idea. But one thing I did know: God was my priority, and if that meant moving, that's exactly what I would do.

The night before my move, I invited David to dinner at the Blue Ridge Grill, my thank you gift for his help. I was hoping he would say that he'd like to visit me in Charlotte, but he didn't. It was like two friends having dinner together. I didn't know what to make of it, and I didn't want to get hurt.

On moving day, August 18, 2011, Katie came to my house to say goodbye. She stayed for hours until the moving van was completely loaded. She hugged my neck and had tears in her eyes. I didn't understand why she felt so attached. We had only met one time before. But I felt like my heart was ripping out of my chest as well. I adored her.

If David and I were to become a couple, the odds were nearly insurmountable. It would only happen if God was behind it. I was OK with whatever happened, and there was no way I would pursue a relationship. If David wanted me, he would have to come get me.

CHAPTER 12

Waiting on God

With boxes piled high in my new house, longtime friends in Charlotte helped me tackle the unpacking. Not long into the task, one friend shouted, "Hey, Claudia. I think you better come see this!"

In her hand was a note she found in one of the boxes labeled "kitchen." As she peered over my shoulder, I opened the envelope. Astonished, I began to read the following:

> Claudia,
>
> I'll bet all of your friends in Charlotte are really tired with all of your unpacking. Enjoy! As you set up your new home (beautiful!), it has to be great to know you are there because you are in God's will for this present time. Hurry up and get all of those empty boxes out—I'm ready to come to Charlotte!
>
> Missing you,
>
> David

Neither of us said anything for a nanosecond, and then we started squealing like teenagers! After that, my friends and I were on a mission to find out if there were any more notes. That was the fastest unpacking process known to man! Soon, another note was discovered.

Claudia,

I have had a great time with you the past few weeks. Everything is comfortable when we are together—no stress, but fun; no pretense, just honesty. That really is nice! So, why are you in Charlotte, and I'm in Marietta? I think God has a few things for both of us to do! I plan to learn more about God's love for me and how He can help me heal!

David

I John 4:15–21

My heart felt like it was going to beat right out of my chest! We found one more note. Shocked. Thrilled. Confused. Excited out of my mind. In Wonder. Amazed. Dumbfounded. I can't express all the emotions I was feeling. I hurriedly looked up the Scripture reference David put in his note. It said:

> Whoever confesses that Jesus is the Son of God, God abides in him, and he in God. We have come to know and have believed the love which God has for us. God is love, and the one who abides in love abides in God, and God abides in him. By this, love is perfected with us, so that we may have confidence in the day of judgment; because as He is, so also are we in this world. There is no fear in love; but perfect love casts out fear, because fear involves punishment, and the one who fears is not perfected in love. We love, because He first loved us. If someone says, "I love God," and hates his brother, he is a liar; for the one who does not love his brother whom he has seen, cannot love God whom he has not seen. And this

commandment we have from Him, that the one who loves God
should love his brother also. —1 John 4:15–21

OK. I admit it. I was trying not to read too much into it and get my hopes up, but those verses sure mentioned the word *love* a lot. The few times I saw him before moving were great, but because he never gave me an indication that he thought of me as more than a friend, I truly didn't know what to think. *Giddy.* That's what I felt. I couldn't help it. The cards changed everything.

I wanted to call him, but I waited. I knew he was working. During his lunchtime, however, he called me. I told him that I found the notes and how special they were to me. I could hear the smile in his voice. And I was smiling, too.

I had never kissed Claudia nor even held her hand, but I was totally in love with her. We made a plan for me to visit her in September 2011, once I returned from a vacation with Katie. I knew what I felt in my heart but was unsure how she felt about me. In the meantime, I called her almost every night and wrote her letters until we could see each other in person.

We saw each other briefly in Atlanta in September, when she was returning from vacation with a friend. I planned to pick her up at the airport, but I was an hour late—her flight came in early. I gave her something I had purchased on my vacation. I know I was being quiet because of nerves. Claudia finally asked me, "Do you really want me here?" I said, "Absolutely." Then I got up enough courage to tell her that I thought she was beautiful. She relaxed after that, and so did I. I revealed other things on my heart about us as well.

That night when I was home and she was driving back to Charlotte, I wrote her an email, reiterating that I once thought I would never marry again, but my way of thinking had changed because of her. I wrote, "I want to be sure that you heard me correctly regarding some of the things I said while at the restaurant, so it bears repeating. You are a beautiful woman, and I am proud to have you on my arm walking anywhere, anytime. You are full of energy, therefore, full of life. You make me happy."

I put my heart on the line, but it was time to take this relationship to the next level. We made a plan for me to visit her in Charlotte two weeks later.

Before David's visit to Charlotte, I was scared out of my wits. Was this for real? I couldn't believe that he thought I was beautiful. Even when I texted him a photo of my friend and me from my vacation, I thought I looked terrible, and I was so afraid that I considered ending the relationship. My friend told me to stop it. She said, "Don't let your past win."

Some of my friends from Charlotte were dying to meet him, so I reluctantly agreed. I had no clue where this relationship was headed but knew there was a real possibility that my desire for a husband may not be out of reach.

David completely respected both God's Word and me in our relationship. We saw each other every weekend—either he flew or drove to Charlotte, or I traveled to Atlanta to stay with a friend.

In one of the letters he sent me through the postal service, he wrote, "I continue to work on allowing myself to be happy, and when we talk or are together, being happy and relaxed is so much easier than it has been in a long time. I am again thankful for God's love, peace, and healing and for what He is doing for me (and I hope you, too!) through our relationship." David still needed healing after Kelly's death, and I know we were both healing from past pain.

By October, I was falling in love with David. I had not encouraged kissing or holding hands. I think he was waiting on me. We were in the car one weekend, and I mustered up the nerve to ask, "Can you drive with your left hand?" He looked at me strangely and responded, "Yes." So I said, "Let me have your right hand then." That's the first time we held hands.

Not long after, we confessed our love to one another. We both discussed the incredible peace we felt. We knew it was God's peace.

During the weekdays, we talked on the phone, emailed, and David sent me numerous little gifts in the mail, like Carolina Panthers paraphernalia. He sent something similar to what we saw at the craft fair in Chattanooga. He called it a "rock in a box," but it was actually a rock with a candle on it that was fueled by oil. It was *different*, but it was a gift from the man I was quickly falling for. He continued to surprise and woo me as the relationship progressed. Each day, I ran to the mailbox to see if there was anything from him. I also checked my email the moment I woke every morning.

All I wanted was God's man for me, and if David wasn't that person, I wanted God to take him out of the picture. So I surrendered David and our relationship every night on my knees in prayer to God. I knew I would not have the strength to give him up. God would have to remove him if it was not to be. I truly wanted God's will. I had to trust Him.

Back in August, even before Claudia had moved, I told Katie about Claudia, asking her if it was OK to date her. I wanted her approval. Katie was all I had left, and it was important to know what she thought. She gave me her blessing.

When I received this email from Claudia in October, my heart soared. There was no doubt in my mind that she was the one God was bringing into my life. The email said:

Dear David,

I am going to copy for you something I have had hidden in my Bible for at least 20 years and have read and reread it numerous times. I never gave up on God, never limited His power, and never "put Him in a box." Now, it appears God has given me exactly what I have asked Him for in you. You will understand, once you read this [passage called "Perfect Love," from an anonymous author].

Everyone longs to give himself completely to someone, to

have a deep soul relationship with another, to be loved thoroughly and exclusively.

But God, to a believer says:

"No, not until you are satisfied, fulfilled, and content with being loved by Me alone, until giving yourself totally to Me, to have an intensely personal and unique relationship with Me alone, discovering that only in Me is your satisfaction to be found, will you be capable of the perfect human relationship that I have planned for you.

"You will never be united with another until you are united with Me, exclusive of any other desires or longings.

"I want you to stop planning, stop wishing, and allow Me to give you the most thrilling plan existing—one that you cannot imagine! I want you to have the best.

"Please allow Me to bring it to you. You just keep watching Me, expecting the greatest things. Keep experiencing the satisfaction that I am, keep listening and learning the things I tell you. You just wait, that's all.

"Don't be anxious. Don't look at the things you think you want. You just keep looking up to Me, or you'll will miss what I want to show you! And then, when you are ready, I'll surprise you with a love far more wonderful than you could dream of.

"You see, until you are ready—I am working even this moment to have both of you ready at the same time—until you are both satisfied exclusively with Me and the life I have prepared for you, you will not be able to experience the love that exemplifies your relationship with Me. And this is the perfect love.

"And, dear one, I want you to have the most wonderful love. I want you to see in the flesh a picture of your relationship with Me and to enjoy materially and concretely the everlasting union of beauty, perfection, and love that I offer you with Myself.

"Know that I love you utterly. I am Almighty God. Believe it and be satisfied!"

Call me when you can.

Claudia

It was almost Thanksgiving, and Katie called me to ask if I would cook dinner with her for Thanksgiving. This would be the first time to spend any significant time with Katie as well as David's mother, and I was thrilled for the invitation. We would be getting to know each other while cooking. This was the first Thanksgiving in forever it seemed that I had a sure invitation for this holiday, and it felt good. I spent several on my own or with friends, but now I was included in a family. I was happy.

My one-on-one time with Katie was precious. I was hopeful that my relationship with David was headed toward marriage one day, so I told Katie that around me, she could always feel comfortable to talk about her mother. I lost my own father at 23, the same age Katie was when her mother died. We had a lot in common. While cooking, Katie thanked me for making her dad so happy. I told her that he made me happy, too. She said, "If I could have created someone for my dad, it would have been you to a T." We hugged. With that admission, I felt peace and confirmation that God had indeed brought this wonderful family into my life.

Thanksgiving was a huge success, especially calming any uncertainty about Katie's response to Claudia. We felt like a family, and I think it was an event that helped Katie to continue to heal from losing her mother and sister. My mother, who was with us Thanksgiving Day, loved Claudia!

Before Thanksgiving, I knew that I wanted Claudia to be my wife. Secretly, I started looking for an engagement ring. I made an appointment with a salesperson at a jewelry store. It was about a mile from Claudia's house. One day when I was in Charlotte just before Thanksgiving, I looked at diamonds at that store without Claudia knowing. I bought a diamond and arranged to have it set in a ring. It was then shipped to me in Atlanta where it burned a hole in my pocket.

I wanted to make my proposal special, because Claudia deserved it. And I wanted to propose to her in Atlanta. I invited her to spend Christmas with Katie and me, and my plan was to take her to the top of Kennesaw Mountain near my home and ask her to marry me. But the weather wasn't cooperating. It was a rainy Christmas Day. So on my way to drive her back to Charlotte, I decided to stop at the Marietta Square where our first date occurred on July 1, six months before.

It was cold. I pulled the car into a parking space and didn't say anything for a minute. She looked at me with a question in her eyes and asked, "David, what are you doing?" I told her I wanted to walk around. "OK," she said, probably wondering what in the world had come over me. I rolled up my pant legs, got a big umbrella out of the back seat, and went around the car to open her door.

I guided her to the gazebo on the square, set the umbrella beside me, and taking a deep breath, I got down on one knee.

Oh. My. Goodness. He's getting down on one knee. I'm in blasted workout clothes! Oh, my goodness! This is it. This is the moment I've been dreaming of for a lifetime.

"Claudia," he said, "We've been dating for six months. Would you make it the rest of my life?"

I was so excited. The ring was exactly what I would have picked out. Without hesitation, I told him, "Yes!"

That's our remarkable love story. I felt like this man, the other prince in my life besides Jesus, had slipped the glass slipper on my foot and it fit. He pursued me. He didn't give up. He loved me unconditionally. There were times even during my engagement that I wondered if I was really worthy of David's love. I didn't think I was pretty enough or good enough. That's what Satan wanted me to believe. I even told our premarital counselor my concerns, but David assured me that he wanted me and that I was beautiful. He chose me! It took a while for this reality to sink into my head and reach my heart.

With David, I felt peace. It was if we had known each other 20 years. We could be ourselves. He loved me regardless of my moods or appearance. I did not have to be a size six or jovial all the time. Our relationship brought healing to both of us.

On May 19, 2012, at age 54, I walked down the church aisle to marry the man of my dreams. We had a God-ordained relationship. The moment I started down the aisle, my eyes searched for his. When our eyes connected, David gave me the biggest smile. My gift to him was my purity. No man had taken that from me. David had only known one woman physically, his first wife; I was blessed with a godly man of good character and integrity. David was God's gift and was beyond anything I could have imagined.

Isaiah 64:4 is a verse I had claimed as my wedding verse for at least 30 years: "For from days of old they have not heard or perceived by ear, nor has the eye seen a God besides You, who acts in behalf of the one who waits for Him." I had waited and trusted God for His timing and His man for me. I realize that it doesn't always happen like this for single women. I came to a place of peace years before that, if I stayed single the rest of my life, it was OK. God intended something else for me, however, and that's good, too. He knows what is best for us. He really does.

CHAPTER 13

Unleashing Joy

With the tropical, morning sun inching its way through the curtains, I turned my head slightly on the pillow and glanced at my new husband sleeping serenely in our hotel bed. Trying not to wake him, I watched him and smiled. It was hard not to pinch myself to see if I was dreaming. Peace and love overwhelmed me—this man was a gift God chose to give me.

Our honeymoon in Maui was glorious—ten extraordinary days of beginning life together filled with love, laughter, sightseeing, sports, beautiful beaches and scenery, and total acceptance of each other. At first, I was nervous for my husband to see all of me (all those issues of insecurity about my body surfacing again!), but he gently assured me that he loved every bit and thought I was beautiful. What remained of my uncertainty crumbled, and freedom replaced my doubts.

As I continued to watch him, David opened his eyes and smiled. The goodness of my Father who blessed me with this sweet man was awe-inspiring.

I've now been married more than four years. I've learned that I can occasionally mess up, but David still loves me. He doesn't love me because I'm a certain size or because my hair and makeup are perfect. He loves me even when I'm in a bad mood or sad. There's no worry that he will fall out of love with me or that he will abandon me. I trust God and him. And I love both.

I will admit when we were in our first weeks of marriage, I didn't know him well enough to be this confident. One time, he came home from a long day at work and was quiet. I immediately got frightened that he was falling out of love with me. I asked if he was mad at me and to tell me what was wrong. He said nothing was wrong. That's the thing about perception. Speculation and perception can be totally unfounded. Taking these wrong perceptions captive so that Satan wouldn't deceive me became my challenge. But David proved over and over that his love was unconditional. I had to allow David to be sad at times about his daughter who had died or to unwind quietly after a challenging day at work instead of thinking every little thing was about me.

In many ways, the things I appreciate about David remind me of the things I love about Jesus. Both are forgiving, accepting, compassionate, and loving. But I certainly need to clarify the difference. My husband, as much as I love him and he loves me, will never ever be able to meet all my needs or be the one who fills me with joy. David may make me happy, but only Jesus gives deep joy and contentment. He knows us far more than a husband ever could. Jesus knows us more than we realize—our thoughts, our dreams, our past, our secrets, our sins, and our fears. And He is more than we can comprehend. He is the Son of God, the gate to heaven, the Great Physician, and the Prince of Peace. He calls us to be His followers. He is not our fairy godmother who gives us what we want. He gives us what we need to be like Him. He opens up to us more than we ever wanted and all we really needed. No man can do that. No man can save or rescue us. Only Jesus can. Jesus gives new life.

God's kind of joy is not dependent on circumstances. It's being completely satisfied and fulfilled even when things are tough. Real satisfaction must be in Him, not in people or circumstances. It's realizing that:

> Neither death, nor life, nor angels, nor principalities, nor
> things present, nor things to come, nor powers, nor height,
> nor depth, nor any other created thing, will be able to separate
> us from the love of God, which is in Christ Jesus our Lord.
> —Romans 8:38–39

It agrees with Habakkuk:

> Though the fig tree should not blossom and there be no fruit
> on the vines, though the yield of the olive should fail and the
> fields produce no food, though the flock should be cut off
> from the fold and there be no cattle in the stalls, yet I will
> exult in the Lord, I will rejoice in the God of my salvation.
> —Habakkuk 3:17–18

Joy is saying with Job, "Though He slay me, I will hope in Him" (Job 13:15).

And contentment goes hand in hand with real joy that's from God. Contentment is true fulfillment. When I finally surrendered my desires and dreams to God, fully assured that He would answer them in His timing or that He would remove my desires if they were not in His will, my heart became fertile ground for joy and contentment. Trust and obedience to God are the ways we maintain contentment. Being discontent comes when we take back control of our lives instead of allowing God's Holy Spirit to control us. My clue that I'm discontent is when I start manipulating to get what I want. There's no doubt that I took control of my life in Europe, and the outcome was disastrous.

Praise and thankfulness are fruits of a joyful and content heart. So is the ability to forgive. As much as David, my husband, brings happiness in my life, my earthly prince does not walk on water. He has flaws. Only God is the source of real joy and contentment.

Our sufficiency must be in Christ. He alone brings peace, despite what is going on around us. As we obey Jesus and trust Him with every aspect of life, we experience peace. Following Jesus and obeying His Word, no matter the cost, deepens my relationship with my Savior and fulfills a longing in my life that only He can satisfy. Human relationships, money, a career, marriage, children, and food will never bring contentment like the Prince of Peace.

The Apostle Paul knew about joy and contentment. In Philippians 4, he touches on both subjects. In verses 4–7, he said:

> Rejoice in the Lord always; again I will say, rejoice! Let your gentle spirit be known to all men. The Lord is near. Be anxious for nothing, but in everything by prayer and supplication with thanksgiving let your requests be made known to God. And the peace of God, which surpasses all comprehension, will guard your hearts and your minds in Christ Jesus.

A few verses later, Paul continued:

> I have learned to be content in whatever circumstances I am. I know how to get along with humble means, and I also know how to live in prosperity; in any and every circumstance I have learned the secret of being filled and going hungry, both of having abundance and suffering need. I can do all things through Him who strengthens me. —Philippians 4:11–13

Paul learned joy and contentment in the broken places. He did not become anxious and disturbed, but rather trusted in God and relied on the Holy Spirit who dwelt in him.

Through complete brokenness, I found a close relationship to God. He became my abiding peace, full contentment, and overflowing joy. My affliction was worth it to find God. Some of that suffering was out of my control—due to things that happened to me—but much of it was self-inflicted in my disobedience. Am I more careful to follow Jesus now? Absolutely. God taught me great lessons during my trials and pain—most importantly that He is enough.

It is not easy to go through trials, disappointment, loneliness, or pain, especially when it's a result of life in an imperfect world. I've already mentioned this passage in James, but it's worth mentioning again:

> Consider it all joy, my brethren, when you encounter various trials, knowing that the testing of your faith produces endurance. And let endurance have its perfect result, so that you may be perfect and complete, lacking in nothing.
> —James 1:2–4

Really? How do trials and joy go together? We are not sheltered from pain as Christians. But we can be joyful because we have the Holy Spirit dwelling in us. He is our Helper. Joy focuses on Jesus and not our trials or those who offend us. Faith produces endurance, the ability to remain standing when the trial is over.

Focusing on Jesus is the key to unleashing joy. According to Hebrews 12:1–2, we are encouraged to:

> Lay aside every encumbrance and the sin which so easily entangles us, and let us run with endurance the race that is set before us, fixing our eyes on Jesus, the author and perfecter of faith, who for the joy set before Him endured the cross, despising the shame, and has sat down at the right hand of the throne of God.

While crucified on the Cross, Jesus saw what mattered—our salvation. He took all of the world's sin on Himself to make us right with God. It was a joy for Him to know that what He had come to earth to accomplish was completed on the Cross. He rose again, conquering death, and we can have that same resurrection power to give us a new life in Him. Our faith originates in Jesus Christ, and He perfects our faith through trials. My eyes must totally be on Him, my Prince of Peace, instead of myself. Self-sufficiency always gets me into trouble! Focusing on my pain, suffering, abandonment, rejection, rights, or loss got me nowhere. Focusing on Jesus brings joy, contentment, and peace.

In this decade of my fifties, God has been teaching me about praising Him. I can totally relate to Psalm 30:11–12:

> You have turned for me my mourning into dancing; You have loosed my sackcloth and girded me with gladness, that my soul may sing praise to You and not be silent. O LORD my God, I will give thanks to You forever.

If you have experienced brokenness as I have, you may also know that God is all that's left in the end. In that state, only God is able to restore joy and purpose. He can do that for anyone who is willing to yield everything to Him. He gives us His unconditional and sacred love, and He teaches a soft heart how to love others the same way. He shows us that self-loathing is a sick form of pride, but acceptance of His holy love changes everything.

We can all think of a reason to have a victim mentality. Everyone has pain. But when we can't love and forgive others as God has taught us to love and forgive, we lose and Satan wins. Pain and suffering have a way of teaching us about real joy, but only if we choose God's way, as we've seen in the Book of James. God doesn't want us to waste our pain and brokenness; He wants to use it for His glory and for our good.

God does not delight in the bad things that happen to us. We live in a fallen world, and stuff happens. But God does delight in our obedience and choice to be joyful, thankful, and full of praise for Him, even when life is difficult.

To singles or those in difficult marriages, I want to encourage you: God's love is enough. He will meet your needs. Don't believe Satan's lie that you're not attractive enough or too damaged to be loved and accepted. God loves you. He will fill your emptiness. For singles, if it's His will for you to marry, that person will show up in God's timing. Psalm 40:1–3 once again ministered to my weary soul during those three years I waited for David. He heard my cry. He put praise for Him into my mouth.

If you haven't waited patiently on God, cry out to Him and repent of your desire for self-sufficiency and bent toward impatience. In the days of Hezekiah, God spoke to His chosen servant, "I have heard your prayer, I have seen your tears; behold, I will heal you" (2 Kings 20:5). God heals our pain. Psalm 147:3 is one of my favorite verses: "He heals the brokenhearted and binds up their wounds." God sees you. See God as Healer, not as the One we blame for our singleness or poor marriages. His plan for you is good, and His desire is for you to have abundant life in Him, no matter your circumstances.

Why did I have to wait until the age of 54 to marry? I'm not exactly sure, but I suspect that God needed time to teach me to love Him, accept His love, and abide in Him. He wanted me to find true joy and contentment in Him. That's far more important than being married to a man. God wanted to "restore to me the joy of [His] salvation and sustain me with a willing spirit" (Psalm 51:12).

Prince Jesus completely swept me off my feet. He will do that to anyone who comes to Him and asks, whether it's the first time you've considered Jesus or if you want to return to His loving care. He wants all of you. He won't settle for part of you. Joy and contentment can only come when you surrender everything to Jesus. He longs to redeem us. Truly He loves us and says, "I have loved you with an everlasting love; therefore I have drawn you with lovingkindness" (Jeremiah 31:3). That everlasting love describes the Prince of my heart. Jesus longs to do that for anyone who calls upon His name.

Questions to Consider or Discuss

Chapter 1

What does it mean to be the bride of Christ? Compare your idea with Ephesians 5:25–27; Isaiah 61:10; 62:5; and Revelation 19:6–8.

Have you experienced brokenness? If so, explain how God used your brokenness to conform you more to His image.

Think of someone who is going through a difficult time. How can you reach out to that person and show compassion?

Chapter 2

Have you surrendered everything in your life to God? Have you given Him your rights? If you haven't, what do you need to surrender?

What thoughts do you need to "take captive"? What Scripture can you use to defeat Satan concerning these thoughts?

Read Ephesians 6:10–17. Make a list of each piece of armor and its purpose.

Chapter 3

Make a list of any dreams or desires you have that are not yet fulfilled.

Have you limited God or "put Him in a box" concerning unfulfilled dreams or desires? If so, explain how you have done that.

Write a prayer to God concerning your desires and dreams that have not yet been fulfilled.

Chapter 4

Who has been most influential in how you view yourself? How do you view yourself?

Think of a time(s) in your past in which your plans or hopes were destroyed. Explain how you felt and how it affected you.

Describe how you believe God views you. Can this description be supported with Scripture? If so, give examples. Ask God to reveal His pleasure toward you and His love for you.

Chapter 5

Name some areas in your life where you have felt "not good enough."

In what ways have you put up walls to protect yourself?

Read and meditate on Psalm 139:13–18. What is God saying to you through this passage?

Chapter 6

What significant event(s) in your life, good or bad, set you in a different direction? How did that event(s) impact your feelings about God?

What bondage in your life has kept you in isolation? What reason(s) can you give for not dropping these heavy weights or how have you gotten past them?

Write out a prayer to God asking Him to free you from any lingering bondage that prevents you from living an abundant life in Christ.

Chapter 7

Has there ever been a period of time in your life when you deliberately disobeyed God? What were some significant consequences of your choices?

Explain how God has tested your faith.

What steps can you make to change your tendencies to do things your own way instead of God's way?

Chapter 8

What does God's Word say about forgiving others? How is God speaking to you through His Word about forgiving others?

Have you chosen not to forgive someone? Why? If so, confess this to God. If you're not sure, ask God to reveal to you anyone you need to forgive.

Is there anyone that you have wronged from whom you need to ask forgiveness? Ask God to give you the courage to do so in a timely manner.

Chapter 9

What does God want you to do that may be out of your comfort zone? Is there anything that is keeping you from doing this?

Read 1 Thessalonians 5:24. How can you apply this verse to something God has asked you to do?

Have you ever gone on a missions trip? If so, how did it change your life? If not, ask God to show you if this is something He wants you to do.

Chapter 10

Think about a time when you were disappointed. Did you find yourself stuck in disappointment for a while? Can you think of any verses in the Bible that might help you during times of disappointment?

Have you experienced the loss of a loved one? If so, did it paralyze you for a while? What eventually helped you to get out of a numb state?

Write down your favorite Bible verse about patience.

Chapter 11

When in your life have you been more loyal to God than to your desires? How did He bless you for that loyalty?

What is your love story with Jesus? Share it with someone this week.

What makes you happy? Why?

Chapter 12

Think of one person you love. Why do you love this person?

Think of God's love. How does He love you according to His Word?

How can you share God's sacred love with another person this week?

Chapter 13

What does joy look like in your life? If you have lost your joy, go to the Father in prayer, and ask Him to restore it.

How can you be content in any circumstance?

If God took everything in your life that you hold dear—your family, your reputation, your health, your finances, your material possessions—in order for you to know Him better, would it be worth it? Why or why not?

Appendix—How to Know God

As you read Claudia's story of grace, perhaps you realized that you don't have a personal relationship with God. Claudia shared how she saw God's presence in her life: guiding, leading, and comforting her in times of joy and pain. God loves you deeply and wants you to know Him. He wants to give you purpose and joy in life as you live for His kingdom.

Please take a moment to read and consider the following Scriptures. They will guide you to a deeper understanding of God's plan and demonstrate how you can submit to God's leadership and receive the salvation offered in Christ alone.

Salvation: What Has Jesus Done?

> "Now I make known to you, brethren, the gospel which I preached to you, which also you received, in which also you stand, by which also you are saved, if you hold fast the word which I preached to you, unless you believed in vain. For I delivered to you as of first importance what I also received, that Christ died for our sins according to the Scriptures, and that He was buried, and that He was raised on the third day according to the Scriptures" (1 Corinthians 15:1–4).

It All Begins with a Right Understanding:

Of God and Creation

"In the beginning God created the heavens and the earth" (Genesis 1:1).

"God created man in His own image, in the image of God He created him; male and female He created them" (Genesis 1:27).

"Worthy are You, our Lord and our God, to receive glory and honor and power; for You created all things, and because of Your will they existed, and were created" (Revelation 4:11).

"Everyone who is called by My name, and whom I have created for My glory, whom I have formed, even whom I have made" (Isaiah 43:7).

Of the Fall

"Therefore, just as through one man sin entered into the world, and death through sin, and so death spread to all men, because all sinned" (Romans 5:12).

"For as in Adam all die, so also in Christ all will be made alive" (1 Corinthians 15:22).

Of Jesus as Creator and Redeemer

"'Worthy is the Lamb that was slain to receive power and riches and wisdom and might and honor and glory and blessing.' And every created thing which is in heaven and on the earth and under the earth and on the sea, and all things in them, I heard saying, 'To Him who sits on the throne, and to the Lamb, be blessing and honor and glory and dominion forever and ever'" (Revelation 5:12–13).

Of Jesus and His Death

"For God so loved the world that he gave his one and only Son, that whoever believes in him shall not perish but have eternal life" (John 3:16 NIV).

"He was delivered over to death for our sins and was raised to life for our justification" (Romans 4:25 NIV).

"But God demonstrates his own love for us in this: While we were still sinners, Christ died for us" (Romans 5:8 NIV).

Of Self

"There is no one righteous, not even one; there is no one who understands; there is no one who seeks God. All have turned away" (Romans 3:10–12 NIV).

"For Christ also suffered once for sins, the righteous for the unrighteous, to bring you to God" (1 Peter 3:18 NIV).

Why the Gospel of Jesus Is Unique

- The gospel *does not* say: If I can do a certain thing or be a certain way, God will accept me.

- The gospel *does* say: God accepts me because of Jesus' righteousness. Because of God's love for and acceptance of me, I gladly follow His leadership and strive to walk in a way that pleases Him.

"For by grace you have been saved through faith; and that not of yourselves, it is the gift of God; not as a result of works, so that no one may boast" (Ephesians 2:8–9).

How Do I Become a Christian?

- You must have faith in Christ alone for what He has done on your behalf.

"This righteousness is given through faith in Jesus Christ to all who believe" (Romans 3:22 NIV).

"I do not nullify the grace of God, for if righteousness comes through the Law, then Christ died needlessly" (Galatians 2:21).

- You must turn away from your sins (the acts that God says separate us from Him, the acts that are contrary to God's holy nature and are not good for us).

"I preached that they should repent and turn to God and prove their repentance by their deeds" (Acts 26:20 NIV).

"And He Himself bore our sins in His body on the cross, so that we might die to sin and live to righteousness; for by His wounds you were healed" (1 Peter 2:24).

- Submit to God's guidance. Agree with Him that His ways are better, and you'll purpose to do what God says is right.

"If you confess with your mouth Jesus as Lord, and believe in your heart that God raised Him from the dead, you will be saved" (Romans 10:9).

Be Sure to Count the Cost

> "For which one of you, when he wants to build a tower, does not first sit down and calculate the cost to see if he has enough to complete it?" (Luke 14:28).

• God is more holy that you can imagine; we are more sinful than we will ever admit.

> "Seek the LORD while He may be found; call upon Him while He is near. Let the wicked forsake his way and the unrighteous man his thoughts; and let him return to the LORD, and He will have compassion on him, and to our God, for He will abundantly pardon" (Isaiah 55:6–7).

Where Do I Go From Here?

• Confess and repent: Agree with God about your fallen condition and His plan for redemption.

• Receive: Ask Christ to enter and rule your life.

• Follow: Commit to obey because you are fully accepted by God. Tell a Christ follower who you know about your newfound faith, and connect with a local, Bible-believing body of Christ followers to learn and grow to become more like Jesus.

Adapted from the book *Compelled* by Ed Stetzer and Philip Nation.

EMBRACING
His Love
FOR YOU...

Divine Love
Women Who Have It and How You Can Too
Sally Miller
978-1-59669-415-6
$15.99

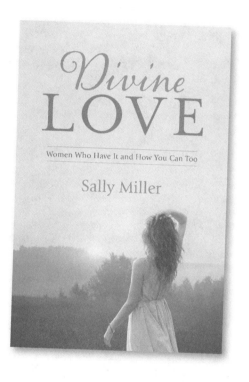

Women everywhere—regardless of age or background—want to experience a life-altering, gentle, everyday kind of love. For years now we have looked at bars, yacht clubs, churches, synagogues, casinos, farmer's markets, dating services, and the Internet trying to find it. Just when we think we have it, we discover that nothing can offer the kind of love our hearts hunger for. How is it that some women through history and today seem to have found the love we all so desperately seek?

Through the remarkable stories of women such as Joan of Arc, Julian of Norwich, Pocahontas, the woman of Endor, Harriet Tubman, Xio Min, and more, women will see extraordinary love can be experienced when seeking it from the Divine.

To read a sample chapter or learn more about New Hope books, visit NewHopePublishers.com.

NEW HOPE®
P U B L I S H E R S
Gospel-Centered. Missions-Driven.

GIVE A GIFT *of Hope!*

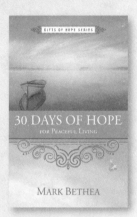

30 Days of Hope for
Peaceful Living
Mark Bethea
978-1-59669-437-8
$9.99

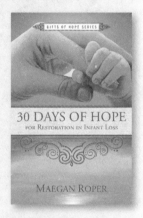

30 Days of Hope for
Restoration in Infant
Loss
Maegan Roper
978-1-59669-438-5
$9.99

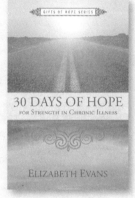

30 Days Hope for
Strength in Chronic
Illness
Elizabeth Evans
978-1-59669-465-1
$9.99

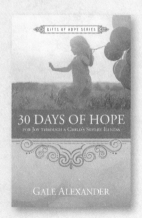

30 Days of Hope
for Joy through
a Child's Severe
Illness
Gale Alexander
978-1-59669-475-0
$9.99

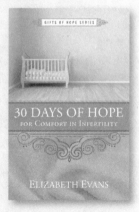

30 Days of Hope for
Comfort in Infertility
Elizabeth Evans
978-1-59669-464-4
$9.99

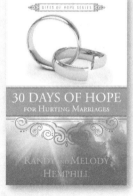

30 Days of Hope for
Hurting Marriages
Randy and Melody
Hemphill
978-1-62591-507-8
$9.99

Use the QR reader on your
smartphone to visit us online at
NewHopePublishers.com.

If you've been blessed by this book, we would like to hear your story. The publisher and author welcome your comments and suggestions at: newhopereader@wmu.org.